THE JOB SEEKER'S HANDBOOK FOR SOCIAL MEDIA
FROM START TO SUCCESS

By George Pond, MA, Ed.

CONTENTS

1. PUT SOCIAL MEDIA TO WORK

PREVIEW

This chapter shows what social media offers for job seeking and career development. Today, you may be unemployed, or enjoying a great job and looking ahead. Social media services can bring further opportunity from any point on your career path.

- Choose social media services that will help create or refine essential job seeking tools.
- Decide on next steps to take to post content and engage in dialog online.
- Choose strategies for networking, developing a professional brand, and boosting your knowledge.
- Know the capabilities of several popular social media services. Choose the services most valuable to your career.

CLAIMING A PLACE

This book is about using social media to find and claim job opportunities. Like billboards and radio ads, social media offers a way to present a message.

If you have a computer or smart phone, you may already be marketing on social media. Does your Facebook profile include work and education information? Have you searched Twitter for job opportunities? How many LinkedIn connections have you made? Your social media experience may be great, or you may just be getting online. Either way, you can boost your career development by setting goals now.

Unlike print and broadcast media, your social media marketing budget can be zero. There is no cost to register and claim a place to bring your messages.

Your online identity, sometimes called a "social media presence", can grow and change. It should. A 21st century career path takes many turns, so job seeking is not a one-time event. On average, people change jobs 11 times[1] between first paycheck and retirement. Sometimes, a change brings the fears and uncertainty of unemployment. Others times, the transition is a solid bridge within the same company.

SELF-MARKETING

On the job or off, most people are job seekers for most of their lives. It begins the first time we knock on an office doors and fill out forms and politely speak with our future employers. Soon after we report to work, job seeking continues as a search for a better job, or for better conditions in a current job. With every task and every meeting we seek opportunity and status at our workplaces. After some months or years, a job seeker who is senior to us (our boss) may give us a promotion, or we find a better job.

We can wait, or we can market ourselves. Our achievements can be known far beyond any corporate confines if we have a blog, and if we post, tweet, pin, and strategically share online.

Our participation online helps us to reach where rewards are found and to gain credentials for what we enjoy. A career path can wind from profession to profession. As years pass, we might have a bit of luck and accrue some money. Then we may retire. Retirement puts an end to the need for self-marketing.

Social Media Planning

Take a moment to consider your current place on a career path. Social media planning begins where you are today, then proceeds to the next job and beyond. What is your current employment status?

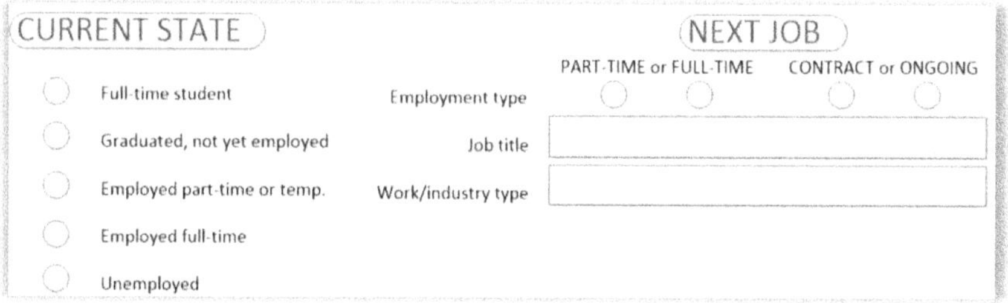

Figure 1 - Job Seeker Status (Current State)

As you proceed from today's current state to your next job, put social media to work for you. Use the capabilities most needed:

o Investigating and exploring new opportunities

You may begin by searching with Twitter keywords or hashtags. A raft of 140-character comments flows down the "Twitter stream"

3

when corporate sales records are set or headquarters move to a new city.

o Networking for greater influence

Regular posts to a blog and Facebook will bring "likes" and "follows". At first, only a few people respond. As you continue to post and Twitter-tweet and Pinterest-pin, that number will grow. You are building an online community.

Keep building. Read the discussions in LinkedIn groups and answer a few profession-related questions. Share comments and bring insight. Your reputation grows with your online community.

o Actively hunting for a job

Job postings appear real-time on LinkedIn and Twitter. Job boards are great and should not be overlooked. Still, social media provides channels for dialog. *Like* and *follow* your favorite companies. Use *comment* functions to ask questions.

Blogging and social media sharing contributes to all of these. From your first day of job seeking until your retirement party, an online presence can enhance your career development.

For today, the only investment is time. Later, when you see results from your investment, you may spend a few bucks on tools and services to market in bigger and faster ways. Getting started is free and it is available now.

PREPARING FOR A JOB SEARCH

The tools of the 20th-century job hunt remain. Most managers want to see a resume; most companies want you to fill out an application. You may be asked for references. A face-to-face interview is usually required. Afterwards, send the obligatory thank you letter.

With 21st-centry technology, cover letters and thank-you's can be cut-and-pasted and delivered faster. Online resumes, job boards, email blasts, and one-click applications extend your reach while increasing the competition.

TOOLS

Which tools will help in your current search?

	HAVE	NEED	DON'T NEED		HAVE	NEED	DON'T NEED
Resume	○	○	○	Print or video portfolio	○	○	○
List of references	○	○	○	Interview tips	○	○	○
Letter formats	○	○	○	Answers to common questions	○	○	○

Figure 2 – Job Seeker Status (Tools)

Consider the tools and strategies you don't have, and those you have but want to enhance. Social media can help you create or refine them.

Which social media services can help you create or refine those tools?

TOOL NEEDED	Facebook	Google+	LinkedIn	Pinterest	Twitter	YouTube
	☐	☐	☐	☐	☐	☐
	☐	☐	☐	☐	☐	☐
	☐	☐	☐	☐	☐	☐
	☐	☐	☐	☐	☐	☐

Figure 3 – Job Seeker Status (Tools Needed)

BEGINNING WITH BLOGGING

This is 21st-century self-promotion. If you are new to it, a blog makes a great first step. Have you already been tweeting and posting and pinning? You, too, should create a blog.

Writing skills are useful, but not required. A blog can begin as an online scrapbook or a loose-leafed portfolio. That's a good start! With more time and content, a blog showcases your expertise through your choice of text, graphics, and video.

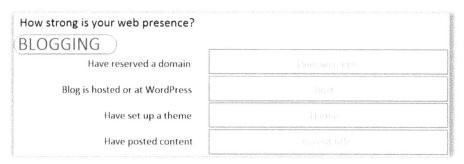

Figure 4 – Job Seeker Status (Blogging)

EXTENDING YOUR REACH

The time you invest in blogging creates richer, longer-lasting content. A tweet is downstream within seconds. Facebook posts may be around for a day or two. A blog is more a more durable way to convey your message. It becomes the hub of your social media outreach. From there, each tweet, pin, and post becomes a spoke that extends out to even greater audiences.

Post to your blog, then copy a link to the short-form content you share through social media services. New readers will follow links to your blog, where more posts and your online profile will boost your strength as a job candidate.

CHOOSING SOCIAL MEDIA SERVICES

The content you create, quote, or re-post beyond blogging reaches users through text, photo, and video-based services. To get started, register with any social media service that might be popular with potential employers:

o Facebook

   Much like a blog, Facebook provides a canvas where 1.2 billion registered users can post text, photo, and video content. Individuals can "like" existing content and create new pages about their interests. Through groups, they can set up an event and with one click invite every member of that group.

   A Facebook page is essential for sharing content to grow an online community.   A Facebook profile is no less essential as it documents your professional brand.

o Google+

   Since its launch in 2011, more than 1.6 million users have registered for Google+. It offers capabilities similar to Facebook, though with a different format. Users can easily create, join, and share content with circles, much like they do with Facebook groups. Through a powerful feature, *hangouts*, anyone with a Google ID can host free videoconferences with up to 10 people in each meeting.

o LinkedIn

   Professionals have replaced their once-popular stack of business cards with the now-essential LinkedIn. The professions range from Acupuncturist to Zookeeper.

Any user can set up a group for their special interest. That interest may be worldwide or focused by geography. Within their groups or by choosing from more than 2 million others, LinkedIn members can post content, review job opportunities, or leave comments.

o Pinterest

The 83%-female population of Pinterest registered users share and comment on photos and videos. This makes a powerful service for sharing visual content about any subject.

Pinterest is not gender-specific or limited by profession. Using convenient tools, anyone can share content from blogs and websites on a pin board.

o Twitter

Most days, about 500 million tweets of 140 characters or less are microblogged through Twitter. Twitter provides timely information about #employment, #careers, or any relevant topic.

Whether they have one or 10,000 followers, users can send Direct Messages (DM) to any follower. They also can post to their entire community of followers through a single tweet.

o YouTube

People who record visual content, include training and sales presentations can edit and share videos through YouTube. For many, the time and effort to prepare YouTube content pays off persuasive impact.

Do you have strong creative and visual skills? Consider recording face-to-face presentations, viewable 24/7 through YouTube. This can be exceptionally powerful if your occupation brings results that are easily seen.

Through social media, you publish without an editor and build reputation and influence through the merit of your ideas. Choose the services in which you can invest time, week after week. It will be an ongoing effort, posting content and engaging with colleagues, leaders, and potential employers.

SOCIAL MEDIA SERVICES

	Facebook	Google+	LinkedIn	Pinterest	Twitter	YouTube
Registered with service	☐	☐	☐	☐	☐	☐
Created profile	☐	☐	☐	☐	☐	☐
Posted recent content	☐	☐	☐	☐	☐	☐
Searching for/engaging with others	☐	☐	☐	☐	☐	☐

Figure 5 – Job Seeker Status (Social Media Services)

The six services featured in this handbook, along with more than 200 others[2], offer social networking that is beneficial to job searches and career development activity.

CHOOSING STRATEGIES

Every job seeker can strategically use social media toward urgent short-term and substantive long-term goals.

o Networking

You may have heard that more than 70% of jobs are filled through networking[3]. Let social media host your everyday job fair and everywhere meet-and-greet. Join in on an anytime happy hour that is free of business casual attire, backslaps, and cold chicken nachos.

Simply provide quality content and engage online. Do this consistently, and your professional network will grow into a lifelong career resource.

o Building a professional brand

Each online profile you create for a social media service defines you for the recruiters and hiring managers who read it. You tell your own story. That story continues when you write a helpful blog post, ask a thoughtful question, or contribute an insightful comment.   The story becomes your professional brand.

o Learning

Social media retrieves opportunities through job title hashtag and keyword searches. A quick visit to LinkedIn, or Twitter reveals which skills are in current demand and which companies are hiring. Visit employers, see their products, and meet their people on Pinterest and YouTube.

Social media is timely. For comparison, take a few books from the shelves of any library. Check the publication dates. Has your profession changed since then? Are employers looking for skills and knowledge that has changed since then?

The networking, professional branding, and learning benefits of Social Media Marketing (SMM) extend through all stages of a career. Whether today you need employment, want something better, hope for a fresh start, or seek that next level of success, use Facebook, Twitter, LinkedIn and other services skillfully and willfully.

SOCIAL MEDIA STRATEGIES

How can you use social media for NETWORKING?

☐ Meet employers ☐ Meet peers/ co-workers ☐ Find opportunities ☐ Share my current status

☐ Meet recruiters/ Human Resource Mgt. ☐ Other: _____

How can you build a PERSONAL BRAND through social media?

☐ Build my reputation ☐ Provide useful content ☐ Post an online portfolio ☐ Show unique skills/ knowledge

☐ Share experiences ☐ Other: _____

What LEARNING is available through social media?

☐ Facts about a trade or profession ☐ Available job boards/ tools ☐ Interviewing tips ☐ Resume formats/ content

☐ Trends ☐ Other: _____

Figure 6 – Marketing Plan (Social Media Strategies)

At first, expect limited yield from these strategies. Long-term, SMM offers great results with no financial outlay. It just takes time.

Most immediate gains are limited to information. Blog and YouTube searches bring technical knowledge. Twitter and LinkedIn searches lead to posted jobs, Pinterest boards preview the places those jobs are found. Companies share their history and culture through Facebook and Google+.

As job seeker, social media can quickly boost your all-essential networking. Even while employed, networking helps. Consider these suggestions:

o Share achievements with your Facebook friends. Post an update about your best day ever at work.

o Build a Google+ circle of human resource and recruiter contacts. Check it frequently to see which jobs they need to fill.

o Start a LinkedIn group for people in your profession. If similar groups exist, focus on your geographic area or one specialty of the job.

o Set up a Pinterest board to display projects you have completed, even if those projects were home-based or done for charity.

o In 140 characters or less, tweet your greatest career strength and a link to a blog post about that career. If unemployed, include the #jobseeker hashtag.

o Outline a YouTube version of your resume. Decide what to say first. Choose whether you will appear on camera or just use presentation slides.

Your self-marketing campaign can begin today. Plan to write content or post a message on each service marked as *registered* in Figure 5. Set a target date. For now, all you only need to write a title or brief description. The completed messages and content will be your first outreach.

FIRST OUTREACH

Social media service	Target date	Message/content to share	(leave blank if not using)
Facebook	/ /		
Google+	/ /		
LinkedIn	/ /		
Pinterest	/ /		
Twitter	/ /		
YouTube	/ /		

Figure 7 – Marketing Plan Worksheet (First Outreach)

Also take a few minutes for initial planning of your ongoing marketing efforts. Do this in pencil. You will want to revisit Figure 8 often, adjusting to reflect the analytics to be discussed in Chapter 6.

In your first look, choose the ones that seem to have the most relevant job and career information. Those should be best for routine reading. Look for services where potential employers and recruiters already participate. That's where you should post. Plan to engage where your knowledge is most likely to be needed, appreciated, and shared.

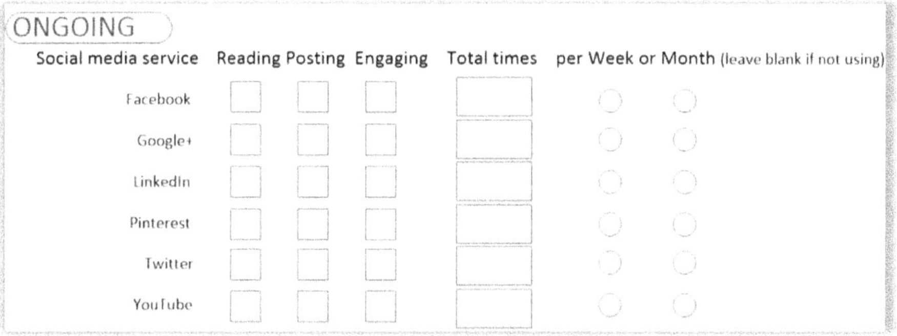

Figure 8 – Marketing Plan Worksheet (Social Media Services)

Within days, you can count *shares* and *follows* on each social media service. On some, your first outreach may be a swing and a miss. On others, you have hit the ball out of the park. Either way, your social media skills will have grown a little stronger.

When you patiently and persistently share good content, your online influence grows. But... expect erosion. Day-to-day, people who needed and liked your blog or LinkedIn group may themselves change professions. They go away. As one rank of followers thins out, prepare to welcome even more people to your online community.

Social Media Marketing is a long-term commitment. Keep posting.

LOOKING AHEAD

Your own efforts will be your greatest investment in Social Media Marketing. Fortune 500 companies employ teams who reach out to customers worldwide. Your community can boost your career, even with fewer than the 2.6 million people following McDonalds on Twitter.

Free power tools can help monitor and schedule social media activity. Other utilities, costing up to $10,000 per year[4] are intended for use by those Fortune 500 marketing teams.

For now, put away your checkbook. Begin at a small scale and watch your online community grow as you invest through these activities:

o Planning.

   So far, we have focused on planning. You now have strategies for putting social media to work.

o Creating a brand

   In chapter 2 you will create a professional brand. To do this, you will first define an online community made up of groups that you want to reach.

o Writing content

   The third chapter presents options for marketing through blogs and social media services. Chapter 4 will help you plan and accomplish the necessary writing.

o Engaging

   Unlike broadcasts and billboards, social media marketing seeks ongoing dialog. Chapter 5 shows how a social media campaign can be more effective. You will learn about power tools as well as strategies for writing content that inspires sharing and comments.

o Measuring

The final chapter gives you tools to measure that success. You can then adjust your social media marketing campaign to sustain success.

Now it's time to recap and to take a short quiz. Every chapter in this handbook has questions with answers that you can check and review as needed. Be assured that you are learning to use social media for job seeking. You have begun the journey from start to success!

CHAPTER 1 RECAP

Social media can be useful from an initial job search through every turn and milestone of a career path. Marketing efforts will provide immediate timely information while, longer-term, you will build a network.

Take a strategic approach. Make a blog the hub of your social media outreach. From there, Facebook, Twitter and other social media services will form the spokes.

Choose social media services that are best for your profession. You can begin by registering on the service and seeing what is posted there, and by home. Decide where future managers and recruiters are most likely to read and share content.

Focus your reading, content posting, and sharing through the services most valuable to you. In implementing your plan, remember that the only necessary investment is time. Patience and perseverance will bring dividends.

CHAPTER 1 QUIZ

1. Which of these is not a valid use of social media?

   a) Investigating and exploring new opportunities

   b) Actively looking for a job

   c) Limiting the need for face-to-face interviews

   d) Networking for greater influence

2. How can a professional build a professional brand?

   a) Contribute helpful, insightful, and thoughtful content through blogs and social media services

   b) Create a website that shows your skills and achievements. Make it easily viewed through smart phones as well as desktop computers.

   c) Identify key professionals. Connect with them on LinkedIn, friend them on Facebook, and follow them on Twitter.

   d) All of the above

3. Which of these statements about Social Media Marketing are true?

   a) It is like a job fair that is held every day

   b) It is like networking, but without the conversation

   c) Both a) and b)

   d) Neither a) nor b)

4. What immediate career help can social media provide?

   a) Recognition, when content is liked, shared, or retweeted

   b) Endorsements from LinkedIn connections

   c) Information found using Twitter hashtags and keywords

   d) Answers to specific questions on a Facebook business page

5. **What do Twitter lists, LinkedIn groups, and Facebook pages have in common?**

   a) They are only available through upgrades

   b) Each requires that you first create a profile

   c) All of them are free

   d) Content written for one can (and should be) posted to all three

6. **Which traits are most needed for online influence?**

   a) Honesty and empathy

   b) Patience and persistence

   c) Focus and persuasiveness

   d) Ability to learn and willingness to share

7. **How can social media marketing help in a job search?**

   a) Share your work achievements with Facebook friends

   b) Join a LinkedIn group for people in your profession, or initiate a new group

   c) Create Google+ circles of human resource and recruiter contacts. Read about the jobs they have to fill.

   d) All of the above

8. **Which strategy brings first results to a job seeker?**

   a) Building a professional brand that is based on your unique skills

   b) Finding opportunity through networking

   c) Sharing your current status with managers and recruiters

   d) Learning about posted jobs and gaining technical knowledge

9. Which investments are essential to a professional's social media marketing?

   a) Subscriptions to tools like HootSuite to better use online services

   b) Time, week after week, in writing content and engaging online

   c) Advertising on Facebook or Twitter to grow your audience reach

   d) All of the above

10. Which is an unlikely result of social media marketing?

   a) Learning of an opportunity ahead of the competition

   b) Defining your one-of-a-kind identity based on experience, skills, and knowledge

   c) Gaining the attention of company owners and executives

   d) Developing a reputation as expert

ANSWERS - CHAPTER 1 QUIZ

1. c   Social media marketing can bring more invitations to face-to-face interviews.

2. a   Your online reputation grows as you post great content and helpfully engage.

3. a   Job seekers can find opportunity through social media at any hour, any day.

4. c   Online responses take time, but social media often leads to the latest information.

5. c   Facebook, Google+, LinkedIn, Pinterest, Twitter, and YouTube all offer free accounts.

6. b   As you persistently write content and engage, you must patiently wait for results.

7. d   Friends, colleagues, and human resource professionals can all be reached.

8. d   Learning begins immediately. Networking and professional brand-building can take longer.

9. b   The best social media marketing investment is time.

10. c   You may not reach executives, but recruiters and managers often use social media.

FORMS IN THIS CHAPTER

Chapter 1 included these forms for putting social media to work:

Job Seeker Status

Marketing Plan Worksheet

Both forms are available in the *Job Seeker's Toolkit for Social Media Marketing*. Download the toolkit free at http://www.wagescope.com. All forms can be copied as needed, subject to terms explained in the toolkit.

2. CREATE A PROFESSIONAL BRAND

PREVIEW

Effective marketing brings a clear message to the right people. Chapter 2 explains how to form an online community of the "right people" to reach. It takes you step-by-step through creating a professional brand. That brand will be the focus of your social media message.

- Plan an online community by identifying groups which can further your career development and job searching. You will share content and engage with them through the social media services that you selected in chapter 1.
- Write an "elevator speech", floor-by-floor.
- Develop a professional brand and a tag line or nickname to represent it. The brand will communicate your unique combination of experience, skills, and professional accomplishments.

BUILDING A COMMUNITY

Social media is simple to use. Social media marketing requires a bit more.

A job seeker could quite easily go to http://www.twitter.com, enter any profession and city name into the "Search Twitter" box. This would be likely to find recent opportunities along with an advertisement (promoted tweet) or two.

For example, a search with "Accountant" and "Joplin" keywords retrieves a stream of Accountant opportunities in Joplin, Missouri.

Screen Capture 1 – Searching for a career, somewhere

That use of Twitter results in learning. The Accountant learns of relevant opportunities in and around Joplin, Missouri. Still, Twitter and other social media offer much more.

You can build an online community to support your job-seeking and career development. Identify characteristics of the people you wish to reach. Target content and social media messages to groups having those characteristics. When they respond, they become part of your online community. They are your network. They, in turn, with target you for employment and career development opportunities.

Your online community might have some groups to support a job seeking goal and others for career development. Several groups can support similar goals. There will be one group for each service. Consider these groups to include in your network:

o Recruiters

   You can limit this to a place, or to recruiters for full-time opportunities. They are likely to be found through LinkedIn.

o Human Resource Managers

   Again, this group or related groups could be specific to a place. For example, *HRMgr_Joplin* and *HRMgr_Galena*.

o People employed where you would like to work

   Use keywords for the company name and places that you want to reach.

Groups can be further defined by the service used to reach them. For example, a group could be defined through Twitter, using a keyword search of *"human resource manager"*. You could abbreviate that group name as *HRMgr_Joplin_Tw*. On LinkedIn, the same keywords would find contacts to tag as a second group, *HRMgr_Joplin_LI*. Few individuals would belong to both groups.

People register for multiple services, but rarely post content to more than one.

Use the *Community Planning Worksheet* to identify groups, where you will find them, and how you will reach them.

TARGETED GROUPS	PLACES	SOCIAL MEDIA SERVICES					
Who can help you find and win the next job?	Where are those groups?	Which services do they most likely use? Facebook Google+ LinkedIn Pinterest Twitter YouTube					
Managers/supervisors		☐	☐	☐	☐	☐	☐
Human Resource Managers		☐	☐	☐	☐	☐	☐
People well-known in the trade/profession		☐	☐	☐	☐	☐	☐
Recruiters		☐	☐	☐	☐	☐	☐
Business owners		☐	☐	☐	☐	☐	☐
Clients/customers		☐	☐	☐	☐	☐	☐
Current co-workers		☐	☐	☐	☐	☐	☐
Future co-workers		☐	☐	☐	☐	☐	☐
Advisors/counsellors		☐	☐	☐	☐	☐	☐
Friends		☐	☐	☐	☐	☐	☐
Relatives		☐	☐	☐	☐	☐	☐
Other:		☐	☐	☐	☐	☐	☐
Other:		☐	☐	☐	☐	☐	☐
Other:		☐	☐	☐	☐	☐	☐

Figure 9 – Community Planning Worksheet

The groups in an online community are unstable. As individuals register on Facebook or Twitter, you may find them in your community. At the same time, others will leave the services you use. A community never posted to with will wither like a neglected plant.

With persistent outreach, a community can be ever-expanding. To nurture growth, write compelling content. Content may be in long-form blog posts or short-form tweets and comments. Regardless of length, compelling content will be shared and your online community will thrive.

Through luck or amazing design, your blog post, comment, or photo may "go viral". More often, growth is measured in months and years.

You can further nurture growth through engagement. Chapter 5 covers the techniques of *how* to engage. Here is *why* you engage: As you answer questions and provide discussion thread insight, people join your online community.

Each time you post or engage, target your message to a group. Consider the hiring managers, looking for "right-fit". Others in your profession want answers to their questions. Help them today, keep in touch next week, and next month they may recommend you for a job before it is posted.

When you focus on a group or groups you limit competition. Your resume on CareerBuilder.com competes with 11.2 million monthly visitors[5]. Set yourself apart by publishing content on your blog. Direct and share content to the groups that you have identified. Relevant content brings individual responses. Fresh content brings repeat visits and further sharing.

GROWING THE COMMUNITY

Fresh, relevant content is essential for an online community. Still, there is more to growth. Let others help you with that. Look for ways to invite participation:

o At the end of a blog post, invite comments or ask a thought-provoking question o Include sharing buttons for Facebook, LinkedIn, and other social media services. Several WordPress plugins automatically add these to each post or to a sidebar widget.

o Install the WordPress plugin for ClickToTweet. This enables you to write messages that readers easily share with their Twitter followers.

LinkedIn provides several tools to boost community growth:

o On LinkedIn, select the Connections menu, then select Add Connections. Choose from the webmail icons on that page. LinkedIn will match names and email addresses and select some or all to receive an invitation to connect.

o Join LinkedIn groups relevant to your profession, goals, and brand. Some groups require membership approval. Once approved, you can easily invite other group members to connect.

o Initiate your own LinkedIn group. Invite connections to join it and to share with their connections.

o Share a home page update with your connections, with the public (all LinkedIn users), or with all LinkedIn or Twitter users.

Every social media service offers unique, effective ways to share. You can send a Direct Message (DM) to any *Twitter* follower that you also follow. On *YouTube*, you can upload videos, write comments, or make playlists for your public channel. As you share, your online community grows.

SETTING YOURSELF APART

Growth is not done for its own sake. Huge numbers of connections and followers do not, in themselves, bring opportunity to knock at your door.

The point of building an online community is to enhance your reputation and influence. Give group members a way to remember you. At critical times, they must know your *professional brand*:

o When job vacancies are being filled

o When candidates are being selected for interviews

o When merit increases are being allocated

o When promotions are being considered

A professional brand sets you apart from the competition. It builds your value and makes you the best person to contact.

Base your brand on specific expertise. Your unique combination of strengths gives you an advantage.

Plan your blog around your professional brand. If you are the Accountant who specializes in Missouri corporate taxes, blog about tax law and Missouri government. Blog regularly. The people you want to reach will be interested. As they read the content you provide and the questions you answer, they will associate you with your brand. Unseen competition may have similar knowledge. They will remain unseen. You, through social media marketing of your brand, will be The Expert.

The all-important brand must be carefully created. To be thorough, start with an elevator speech. An elevator speech is a brand presentation pitched to a captive audience between the first and fourth floor.

You have stepped into the elevator. As the doors close, brag to the executives, business owners, and hiring managers that are jammed into the elevator. Don't make them stare at their shoes. To be interesting, brag artfully:

o Redirect the glory. Instead of "I got straight-A's in Corporate Tax Law," you could say "West Missouri U offers great Tax Law courses. They get into the details. Some of those A's weren't easy."

o Make achievements believable. Say what you did. "Junior year, I finally got into Missouri corporate tax law. I made the Dean's List."

When you plan your elevator speech, first focus on 2-5 strengths. For each of those, recap what you did in the past couple of years. Leave the remaining items blank.

ELEVATOR SPEECH

1st – 2nd floors: Your strengths	Check 2-5 greatest strengths you have proven within the past two years. Briefly describe what you did for the items you checked. Leave the remaining items blank.
☐ Achievements	
☐ Awards/Patents	
☐ Experience	
☐ Skills	
☐ Licenses/Certification	
☐ Professional Training	
☐ Education	
☐ Knowledge	

Figure 10 – Brand Development Worksheet (Elevator Speech/Strengths)

The doors open at the second floor, but no one gets out. The doors close. The executives, business owners, and hiring managers have heard your strengths. Now they want to know about your goals.

Use the next part of your elevator speech to show your career path. Be concise: you have about 15 seconds to describe the journey.

2nd – 3rd floors: Your career path	Continue your elevator speech with positive statements about your progress and current direction.
Where I began:	
What I look forward to:	

Figure 11 – Brand Development Worksheet (Elevator Speech/Career Path)

Third floor. The doors open and again, no one gets out. The elevator ride continues for one more floor. Focus on recent achievements at work. Not recently employed? Prove yourself to be productive and engaged through any of these:

o Volunteer work

o Professional organizations

o An at-home project

o Research

o Education

Whether or not they occurred at work, describe achievements relevant to your profession.

3rd – 4th floors: Your recent achievements		If employed now or recently, describe achievements there. If not recently employed, describe volunteer work or an at-home project.	
When	Where	What you did	The results

Figure 12 – Brand Development Worksheet (Elevator Speech/Recent Achievement)

Now you have an elevator speech. You can share parts of it in 140-character tweets, or pin relevant photos, or include in LinkedIn group commentary. Use keywords from it to search your favorite social media.

Offline, be ready for any serious discussion with management. Know the key points of your elevator speech. Be ready to summarize it. What would you say in a 15-second Super Bowl ad about yourself?

	Summarize the key points of your elevator speech.
Your profession is:	
What shows that you good at it? (based on Floors 1-2)	
What shows your motivation to achieve? (Floors 2-3)	
What have you have done recently? (Floors 3-4)	

Figure 13 – Brand Development Worksheet (Elevator Speech/Summary)

Your personal brand must be memorable. You may have scant seconds to convey a message. You can determine how decision-makers remember you. Are you "The Corporate Tax Law Expert" or are you "Bringing new focus to Joplin's Balance Sheet"?

Create a tag line or phrase that summarizes your unique strengths. Why should you be favored for a job or promotion? Base these easily-remembered words on your elevator speech summary (Figure 13).

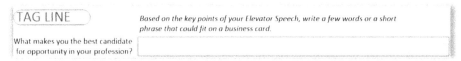

TAG LINE	Based on the key points of your Elevator Speech, write a few words or a short phrase that could fit on a business card.
What makes you the best candidate for opportunity in your profession?	

Figure 14 – Brand Development Worksheet (Tag Line)

As social media marketer, you will find many occasions to reinforce your unique professional image:

o Compress your tag line into hashtags like #TAXACCOUNTING

o Express parts of your elevator speech at length through blog content, or more briefly through posts to Facebook and LinkedIn

o Do you have time and a flair for production? Share your expertise through a series of YouTube videos.

o Your professional brand works just as well offline. Print the tag line on your business card.

DEFENDING YOUR BRAND

Have you ever asked for a "kleenex"? Probably, but the makers of Kleenex® Brand tissues, Kimberly-Clark Corporation, owns registered trademarks which differentiate their brand from other tissues.

Your professional brand will be easier to protect. You won't need corporate attorneys. Just be aware of the one the person most likely to weaken your brand. That person is you.

Most of your competitors have no brand for their job and career development. Even those with an organized social media presence are marketing their own brands. They are unlikely to copy yours.

Be aware of competition, but also know that you can take first place. Defend your brand so that your community remembers you first. Defend it by writing blog posts about key points of your elevator speech. Include your tag line in every online profile. Whenever you engage through a social media service, remember your brand.

BEING THE "RIGHT-FIT"

Your professional brand strengthens as you demonstrate insight and knowledge in blog posts. It represents your one-of-a-kind skillset. The experience and achievements in your online profile provides the detail.

Once your online community associates you with a brand, they have reason to remember you at critical times because you built trust with them:

o You showed interest. You sent DM to Managers who tweeted about job vacancies at their companies.

o You helped. You shared a timely, useful message with others in your profession.

Define a professional brand through social media. Use it in writing the quality content you patiently and persistently share. When it is remembered, opportunity will knock first at your door. You will be summoned as the *right-fit* because you already have shown interest and you already have helped.

CHAPTER 2 RECAP

Focus any job seeking communication toward your online community. Build this community from groups which further your career-long development. Reach out to these groups through the social media services you selected in chapter 1.

Write an elevator speech. Distill the speech into a tag line or short phrase. As you search through social media, use the same words as keywords and hashtags. Frame blog posts around them. Include them in social media messages.

The fresh, relevant content you provide strengthens your unique, memorable professional brand.

CHAPTER 2 QUIZ

1. What is true about the groups in an online community?

   a) A common set of search criteria reaches all of the groups

   b) A online community may be made up of several groups

   c) Most groups can be reached through any social media service

   d) Groups should not be limited by location

2. How might groups be related?

   a) No relationship is likely. Each group can be found through different services, using different keywords.

   b) In an online community, all groups use the same social media service.

   c) Several groups can support similar goals.

   d) Groups have members in common, leaders who participate in the entire online community.

3. How can LinkedIn help to grow an online community?

   a) Connections can be added from webmail accounts

   b) Group members can automatically become connections

   c) Home page updates may be copied to Facebook and Google+

   d) All of the above

4. Which is not a good use of a professional brand?

   a) Reaching a greater variety of opportunity

   b) Enhancing your reputation

   c) Setting you apart from the competition

   d) Making you the best person to contact

5. What is essential to a job seeker's brand?

   a) Covering the full range of experience

   b) Being easy to remember

   c) Bringing attention to specific achievements

   d) Sharing values and commitment

6. What is necessary in writing social media content?

   a) Judgment, to understand what is compelling to people you have never met

   b) Patience, to write longer posts and comments which are more likely to be shared

   c) Persistence, to bring fresh content to an ever-changing online community

   d) Creativity, to find topics that will appeal to a wider audience

7. How can you improve your chances of winning an opportunity?

   a) Demonstrate insight and knowledge in blog posts seen by recruiters

   b) Send Direct Messages to managers who tweet about job vacancies at their companies

   c) Share timely, useful messages with others in your profession

   d) All of the above

8. What is essential to a professional brand?

   a) A phrase or tag line that distinguishes you

   b) A list of skills, education, and experience

   c) A summary of your achievements

   d) A clear next step for immediate action

9. How can you build a reputation as expert and leader in your profession?

   a) Write long-form content in a blog

   b) Share links and timely messages on Twitter

   c) Create a useful series of YouTube videos

   d) All of the above

10. What is communicated in an elevator speech?

   a) Skills, knowledge, and motivation

   b) Interests, abilities, and experience

   c) Training, responsibilities, and commitment to quality

   d) Strengths, a career path, and achievements

ANSWERS - CHAPTER 2 QUIZ

1. b   You may wish to target several groups, including "Colleagues", "Recruiters", and more.

2. c   There may be several goals, with one or more groups associated with each.

3. a   LinkedIn can match names and email addresses in a webmail account with its list of members.

4. a   A professional brand should be specific, not designed for a range of opportunities

5. b   Make your professional brand memorable, so you are the person matched with opportunities

6. c   Fresh, relevant content is essential to sustain an ever-changing online community

7. d   Social media marketing brings opportunity to knock first at your door

8. a   Base all of your online profiles on a phrase or tag line from your professional brand

9. d   All relevant, quality content that you provide strengthens your professional brand

10. d   Your elevator speech describes key strengths, the path you've taken in using them, and what you have achieved as a result

FORMS IN THIS CHAPTER

Chapter 2 included these forms for creating a professional brand:

Community Planning Worksheet

Brand Development Worksheet

Both forms are available in the *Job Seeker's Toolkit for Social Media Marketing*. Download the toolkit free at http://www.wagescope.com. All forms can be copied as needed, subject to terms explained in the toolkit.

3. CLAIM YOUR TERRITORY

PREVIEW

Previous chapters have shown the role of social media marketing at any point in a career, and how to bring focus to that marketing.

Chapter 3 details the social media services essential to job seeking and career development. You will learn to choose and customize services, based on your professional brand. You will plan the foundation for an online presence: your blog.

- Plan a social media profile. The profile should communicate your professional brand.
- Choose a WordPress-hosted or self-hosted blog. Determine which theme best supports the features needed for content you will write.
- You online community is made up of groups. Match these groups to the social media services that you use. Optionally, select free or low-cost tools to automate your online marketing tasks.

Your Social Media Profile

Many social media services include *user profiles*. These profiles provide a great way to reinforce a professional brand.

At any point in any career, you only need one brand. Base your social media profile on that brand. Services do not share profiles with each other, though some will import component parts from others.

Plan a social media profile based on your current professional brand, then update as needed. When configuring each social media service, use components from that profile. It's okay to copy. That makes an easier start in a social media service. It also reinforces your brand.

Several components of a profile are useful on multiple services. Create each component to best present your professional brand:

o Profile picture

Needed for Facebook, Google+, LinkedIn, Pinterest, and Twitter. YouTube uses you Google+ profile picture.

Size, dimensions, and pixel density will varies from service to service. Start with a professional headshot that can be cropped, reduced, and resized as needed. Dress nicely for this photo. Relax, look friendly, and show your pearly whites if you got 'em. If exceptionally camera shy, let an icon of your profession stand in for this picture.

o Cover/header photo

Needed for Facebook, Google+, and Twitter.

On most profile pages, this forms a background for the header. Requirements for size, dimensions, and pixel density vary from service to service. Start with a large image, approximately 1000 x 500 pixels.

To represent your brand, show environments or products easily associated with your profession. Exclude yourself from this picture. Services may superimpose your profile photo as well as some text.

o Work and education

Needed for Facebook. A Google+ "About" page lists Occupation, Skills, and Employment. That information becomes part of your YouTube profile. LinkedIn significantly expands work and education information to form a complete resume.

Your profile should boast of any recent work achievements and prestige employers. If you recall neither of those, mention a career-related project or research that you are doing. Show yourself as productive and positive in some activity, any activity.

Mention your most recent school. If studies focused on your targeted profession, include the degree or certification that you earned. Don't look further back. Your excellent pre-school deportment will not impress a potential employer. Also, you need not include a class year. Dates provide a way to screen you inaccurately, based on perceived experience, and illegally, based on calculated age.

o Contact information

Needed for Facebook, Google+, and LinkedIn. YouTube uses your Google+ profile.

The best possible contact information would be an email address from your personal domain. For example, myfirstname@myfirstandlastname.com. That strategically

41

advertises a self-hosted blog or website while providing a way to reach you.

If you enjoy random commercial outreach including robo-calls, list your telephone number. Otherwise, never post a telephone number on the internet. Opportunity's knock can be communicated via email. For even greater privacy, request a free, unique address through gmail.com, outlook.com, or yahoo.com.

o Bio/About you

Needed for Facebook, Pinterest, and Twitter. On LinkedIn, put this content below "Summary". The Google+ and YouTube "Story" includes a Tagline, Introduction, and Bragging rights.

Make this *about your career*. In chapter 2 you distilled the key points of your elevator speech. Convert them to a short paragraph, add a link to your blog, and your "About you" bio is done.

EFFECTIVE BLOGGING

All of your social media activity can direct an online community to a blog. Link to it from the profile you configure on every service.

A blog can be your personal web page, but is far easier and less expensive to develop than other web content. A blog puts you online in less than an hour. The cost will be free or very low.

Blogs are either *effective* or *ineffective* for job seeking and career development. Planning makes the difference. Start by copying your tag line from chapter 2. List 6 – 8 subjects relevant to your brand. Each should provide interesting topics for a group within your online community.

SUBJECT	Below, fill-in the brand or tag line you have written.		
Your brand/tag line:			

Next, choose 6 – 8 of your targeted groups

Group name	Subjects that would interest them	Relevant to your brand? Y/N	Interesting to you? Y/N
		☐	☐
		☐	☐
		☐	☐
		☐	☐
		☐	☐
		☐	☐
		☐	☐
		☐	☐

Figure 15 – Blog Options Worksheet (Subject)

BLOG HOSTING

Stylecaster.com, itself a blog, suggests "The 10 Best (Free!) Blog Sites[6]". The ten items are in alphabetical order. That places WordPress at the bottom, though it is more popular than any of the others.

More than 74 million[7] blogs have been developed on the WordPress platform. Despite the large number, they are not cookie-cutter, due to the hundreds of free themes, each customizable many ways.

WordPress blogs may be hosted two ways: on WordPress.com, or as a *self-hosted* blog.

WordPress.com blogs are free, with some limitations. A $99 per year upgrade allows the blogger to use any domain name as the web address. For example, the free blog might be at http://wordpress.com/socialmediapro. The upgraded blog would be reached through http://socialmediapro.com. Free "wordpress.com" blog may show ads, and do not permit use of *plugin* software tools. Substantial file space, up to 3 gigabytes, is stored free. Upgraded blogs get an additional 10 gigabytes of storage.

WordPress.com hosts millions of blogs. Millions more are self-hosted through GoDaddy.com and many other web host companies. Starter rates for self-hosted blogs are likely to be less than $10 per month. Often, bloggers paying one year in advance receive additional discounts. The cost should include cPanel or a similar tool that make it easy to install the WordPress program and related files.

Which type of hosting would best meet your blogging needs and budget? Consider the popular options for WordPress:

HOSTING		
Choose either option for hosting:	WordPress.com	cPanel hosting (self-hosting)
Hosting cost	Free	$36 - $84/year
Use your own domain name (.COM)	$17/year	included
Remove external ads	$29.97/year	included
Enhance by using plug-ins	not available	1000's available (many free)
Ability to advertise	Requires approval	included

Figure 16 – Blog Options Worksheet (Hosting)

If you choose WordPress.com to host your blog, create an account at http://www.wordpress.com. Otherwise, you may use a domain (web address) that you have already registered, or you may register a new domain name. GoDaddy offers domain registration as well as web hosting. Registration reserves the domain name, such as *socialmediapro.com*, for 1 year or longer. Web hosting assigns the domain name to a web server where you can install WordPress and your blog.

Your next step in planning a WordPress blog is to choose a theme. WordPress.com offers 99 free themes[8], with more are available by upgrade. Self-hosted blogs have an even greater selection. Thousands[9] of themes are available. If you choose a *responsive* theme, it will automatically format for smart phones and tablets as well as desktops. This makes your blog as readable on a 5-inch touch screen as it is on a 22-inch monitor.

All of these themes are responsive:

THEME	WordPress.com users can choose from 99 free themes. More are available by upgrade. http://theme.wordpress.com/themes/features/responsive-layout/?sort=free
Appliance	Minimalist; rows of rectangles; each post has an image at the top
Bonpress	Left-hand navigation; sidebar widgets
Glider	Text-only
Great	Varied color schemes; Search-Engine Optimized; custom widgets
Hueman	Varied layout options including left and/or right sidebar; Includes slider
InterStellar	Varied layout options
Skeleton	Minimalist
Thoughts	Minimalist; features a large image
vFlex	Includes a slider and import/export capability
Zenith	Varied layout options; magazine-style

If you have cPanel hosting, you can choose from hundreds of additional free themes. http://www.creativeblog.com/web-design/free-wordpress-themes-712429

Figure 17 – Blog Options Worksheet (Theme)

Theme installation includes a sample post. You will replace the sample with content that you plan in chapter 4.

BLOG MARKETING

A blog can affordably market a professional brand, but you have other options. You could rent a billboard never seen by hiring managers on other roads. You could buy a radio spot, unheard by executives tuned to another station. Sadly, you also could create an excellent blog and tirelessly post content to the vast space of the internet.

A blog is a marketing tool which, itself, must be marketed. Social media services do that marketing. You can use any or all of them at no cost. Each message can link to your blog.

Each of these services has reached millions by offering distinct advantages over the others.

SOCIAL MEDIA SERVICES						
	Facebook	Google+	LinkedIn	Pinterest	Twitter	YouTube
Primary content	Text, photos and video	Text, photos and video	Text and photos	Photos	Text	Video
# of users	1.3 billion	540 million	259 million	48.7 million	271 million	1 billion
Focus	Sharing with friends	Sharing with friends	Professional networking	Women (80%), photo albums	Sharing news and events	How-to, movies, TV
Tools	HootSuite Klout	HootSuite	HootSuite Klout	HootSuite	HootSuite TweetAdder	HootSuite (add-in)
Advantages to Job Seekers	Reach, varied content	Reach, varied content	Recruiters, networking	Visual, easy to share	Current, popular	Demos
Time commitment	Flexible	Flexible	Flexible	Flexible	Minimal	High

Figure 18 – Services Options Worksheet (Social Media Services)

In earlier chapters, you chose social media services to promote your job seeking and career development. Now match those services with the groups you defined in chapter 2. Select just one service on each row. If similar groups can be reached through more than one service, create multiple groups. For example, to reach recruiters through both LinkedIn and Twitter, you might have groups named *Recruiters_LinkedIn* and *Recruiters_Twitter*.

Which services would best reach the groups you have targeted? Choose one group and one service on each line. If a group would use two services, split that group into two.						
Group Name	Facebook	Google+	LinkedIn	Pinterest	Twitter	YouTube
	○	○	○	○	○	○
	○	○	○	○	○	○
	○	○	○	○	○	○
	○	○	○	○	○	○
	○	○	○	○	○	○
	○	○	○	○	○	○

Figure 19 – Services Options Worksheet (Groups and Services)

CONFIGURING SOCIAL MEDIA

The popular social media services provide ways to complete to immediately log-in. With some, only an email address is required. Some create credentials from data shared with another service. For example, you may be able to "login with Facebook".

Some services ask you to create a password. Unique passwords are always a good idea. Use a password vault to track these. The PC Magazine "10 best[10]" are available free or at low cost.

Once you have logged-in, you can tweet, post, or otherwise produce content through that service. Your profile will be blank. Take a little time to complete it. A blank profile offers nothing to the people wanting to know more about you.

Invest a few minutes in replacing the default icon and blank descriptions that initially represent you. Consider adapting components of your social media profile (discussed earlier in this chapter) to share your professional brand. That will increase "likes" and "shares". Your online community will grow.

After completing a profile, you can further configure each service to selectively share your posted content:

o Facebook offers dozens of settings[11]. Options are likely to change, but make careful selections within the Privacy category to control your professional brand. Use audience selection capabilities to limit who can see what you post. Limit who can tag you in a photograph.

If you have posted political view or other comments you would ordinary not share with an employer, consider creating a Facebook page for job seeking and career purposes. The page becomes a distinct part of your Facebook account, with separate privacy options. Access can be limited to groups that you specify.

o Google+ provides an elegant way to filter views for your online community. Create a circle for each group. When you post, select circles to view that content, or post it publicly. As your circles grow, consider adding a page for your professional brand, then grant access to your online community circles.

o Your LinkedIn account should focus on career and be viewable by your colleagues, recruiters, and future employers. All of these people should be connections.

When new to LinkedIn, use the built-in tools to import contacts from webmail services. From that list, choose who you would invite to be a connection.

o Set up Pinterest boards for any groups in your online community who favor visual content. A Pinterest account can have up 500 boards, each with thousands of pins. Pins can be expanded to 736 pixels wide.

To limit access to a board, designate it as secret and invite only the individuals you wish to see it.

o Twitter lets you follow at least 2,000 users, but no more than 1,000 per day. As more users follow you, the maximum you can follow is extended.

Security and privacy options[12] restrict other users from deleting tweets on your account. You can block photo tagging and determine whether or not a location will be added to your tweets. Flexible configuration options will format mobile phone text and email messages.

o YouTube works as an extension to Google+. Most configuration is shared, but you must also create a YouTube channel before leaving comments, making playlists, or uploading videos. This can be a personal channel, with your name, or a channel under another name, such as your brand. Each channel you create also initiates a Google+ page.

CHOOSING POWER TOOLS

An online community grows as content is researched and posted, week after week. A one-time effort produces little or nothing.

For long-term results, bring fresh content to your community each day. That presents a challenge. Everyone needs days off and vacations. If content is to be fresh day-and-night, every day, it must be scheduled in advance. Free and low-cost power tools can deliver social media posts at the times you choose.

The same power tools can also help with social media research. Whether you write original content or repost what others have written, you must gather information.

HootSuite, Klout, and TweetAdder schedule posts in advance. Those three, along with Topsy, help in finding existing or in planning original content. Listly is for sharing, not scheduling. TweetAdder will help you decide who to *follow*, and know who does or does not *follow back*.

Social media marketing works on any budget. The popular tools offer free evaluation, some limited by time, and others by excluding some functions:

POWER TOOL STRATEGY

Optionally, choose power tools to work with the social media services you selected.

Power Tool	Facebook	Google+	LinkedIn	Pinterest	Twitter	YouTube
☐ HootSuite	☑	☑	☑		☑	Using add-in
☐ Klout	☑				☑	
☐ Listly	☑	☑	☑		☑	
☐ Topsy					☑	
☐ TweetAdder					☑	

Figure 20 – Services Options Worksheet (Power Tool Strategy)

EXTENDING MARKET REACH

A social media marketing budget might also include advertising and promotion. These could be useful early, mid-career, or late in a career:

o After graduation, Facebook advertising will target a post to employers in a chosen profession

o LinkedIn offers premium services to "stand out to hiring managers", "get in touch with recruiters", and "compare to other candidates" when unemployed

o A promoted Twitter account can lead web traffic to a new blog and reinforce a professional brand.

Social media marketing can be automated and made faster. Its reach can be extended at key points in your career. That much depends on your budget. Most social media marketing is free. Results are achieved through posting and engaging, with or without spending.

CHAPTER 3 RECAP

Promote your professional brand through a blog and every social media service you use. Begin with common profile components that are based on your elevator speech and tag line, written in chapter 2. These components, along with a professional photo and your contact information are essential to each social media profile. Also include them on your blog's "About" page.

The most popular blog platform, WordPress, can be hosted free at WordPress.com or self-hosted for less than $10 per month. Self-hosting with cPanel support enables use of plugins and offers more free themes to customize the layout, fonts, and features.

Most members of your online community will reach your blog through social media services like Facebook, LinkedIn, and Twitter. You may occasionally wish to promote content through paid advertising. More often, time is the essential investment. Be sure to complete a profile on each service. That will enhance your professional brand and lead more people to your blog.

CHAPTER 3 QUIZ

1. On a Wordpress.com blog, which feature requires a $99/year upgrade to Premium?

   a) Up to 3.0 gigabytes of file space

   b) Ability to install free plugins and widgets

   c) Hundreds of free themes

   d) Mobile apps for iOS and Android phones and tablets

2. How can paying for a self-hosted blog help your job search?

   a) More than 10,000 themes are available, for the exact format and style you want to show prospective employers.

   b) You can install plugins to display your Facebook and Twitter activity.

   c) If you already have a website with resume and job samples, you can add a self-hosted blog to it.

   d) All of the above

3. Which is a limitation of a WordPress-hosted blog?

   a) Ads will be included on your blog unless you pay to upgrade.

   b) Custom domain names (such as myblog.com) are not allowed.

   c) Search Engine Optimization (SEO) is not supported.

   d) It is possible but difficult to link to external websites.

4. How can hosting companies simplify installation of the WordPress program and related files?

   a) Providing cPanel or a similar utility

   b) Enabling (File Transfer Protocol) FTP access to the domain

   c) Placing WordPress themes in self-extracting files

   d) All of the above

5. Who is best to invite as LinkedIn connections?

   a) Colleagues, recruiters, and future employers

   b) Leaders and experts in your career field

   c) Professionals with similar backgrounds and experience

   d) People who post quality content in LinkedIn groups

6. What limit does Pinterest set?

   a) Expanded pins can be up to 600 pixels wide

   b) Maximum length for a caption is 256 characters

   c) Up to 20 photos can be pinned to any board

   d) An account may have up to 500 boards

7. What should a person do on Facebook when unemployed?

   a) Temporarily disable the Facebook account

   b) Assign any business and professional contacts to a list. Exclude that list from personal posts.

   c) Create a Facebook group for business and professional contacts

   d) Create a Facebook page for job seeking and career purposes

8. What is required before uploading a video to YouTube?

   a) Logging in with a Gmail (Google mail) account

   b) Creating a YouTube channel

   c) Registering as a contributor

   d) All of the above

9. What should you include in a Twitter profile?

   a) A header photo that represents the product or goals of your profession.

   b) A short bio which includes a link to your blog.

   c) For a profile photo, use either an icon of your profession or a "head shot"

   d) All of the above

10. What is best done using HootSuite, Klout, or TweetAdder?

   a) Importing contacts from webmail services

   b) Creating Twitter lists for an online community

   c) Configuring a consistent online profile

   d) Pre-scheduling tweets to be sent out during a vacation

ANSWERS - CHAPTER 3 QUIZ

1. b   Plug-ins and widgets can only be installed on Premium or self-hosted WordPress blogs.

2. d   A self-hosted WordPress blog offers more choices of how the blog looks and functions.

3. a   A paid upgrade allows domain names can be associated. Ads may display on a free blog.

4. a   With the cPanel utility, click the WordPress icon to begin installation.

5. a   Be sure that colleagues, recruiters, and future employers are aware of your professional brand.

6. d   A Pinterest account can have 500 boards, each with thousands of pins up to 736 pixels wide.

7. d   Facebook pages have separate Privacy options which can limit access to specific groups.

8. b   A YouTube channel is required before leaving comments, making playlists, or uploading videos

9. d   Keep your professional brand in mind as you choose the header photo and write your bio.

10. d   HootSuite, Klout, and TweetAdder can schedule posts in advance.

FORMS IN THIS CHAPTER

Chapter 3 included these forms for choosing among the options provided by social media:

Blog Options Worksheet

Services Options Worksheet

Both forms are available in the *Job Seeker's Toolkit for Social Media Marketing*. Download the toolkit free at http://www.wagescope.com. All forms can be copied as needed, subject to terms explained in the toolkit.

4. POST CONTENT FOR YOUR COMMUNITY

PREVIEW

Social media outreach brings results based on value that it brings to an online community. Chapter 4 guides you through choosing relevant topics and planning quality content. As your online community discovers and shares the content, your professional brand becomes more clearly and widely known.

- Develop topics for blogging or social media posts. To do this, categorize the subjects that you identified in chapter 3. List several topics for each category.
- Plan an original blog post. Begin by choosing one item from your topic list. Research the content. Determine how to best present the topic to reinforce your professional brand.
- Share content through your blog and social media services.

REACHING OUT

You have identified an online community and chosen which social media services to use. That leaves the ongoing task of reaching that community. What content do you post to them today, next week, and a year from now?

Begin by revisiting the subjects that would interest groups in your community. Copy the list from the Subject List form (Figure 15 in chapter 3). Use the column at right to group them into categories. As you list categories, record category numbers to the left of each subject.

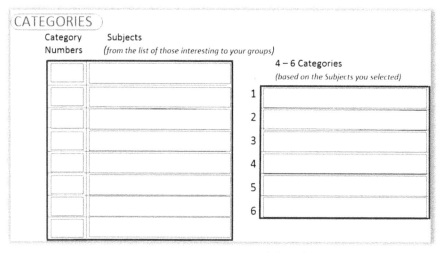

Figure 21 – Content List Worksheet (Categories)

CREATING A TOPICS LIST

Your online community will flourish or wither, depending on how consistently you provide content for them. Ideally, you should write a blog post each week. Twice weekly is even better. Fresh content will encourage people from your online community to return, week after week, and to let their friends and colleagues know about posts they find most useful. If people return and find no new content, that may be their last visit.

Create a topic list to spark your writing week after week. Turn to the list so that you begin with an idea rather than a blank page.

You can also use the list to balance emphasis between categories. Regular coverage of each category is more likely to reach each group. Focus on just one or two, and some groups will respond while others look elsewhere across the web.

Figure 22 – Content List Worksheet (Topics)

PLANNING A BLOG POST

When group members find fresh, quality content on your blog they will share it with their colleagues and friends. For best results, have that content ready for them each week.

Begin with a visit to your topic list. If new topics come to mind, add them to the list. The topics you add may not be the best choice for the current week. Ideally, you should choose from a category not recently covered.

Figure 23 – Blog Post Planning Worksheet (Topic)

With a topic in mind, jot down an outline. Your finished blog post may be just a sentence or two about each point on that outline. Most blog posts are brief. Many blog themes provide wide margins, with generous spacing between lines and paragraphs.

Think about online content you have seen. How much scrolling did it take to reach the bottom of the page? Did subheads, quotes, graphics, and charts fill out the page? Using some of those techniques, you may write less than a half dozen short paragraphs.

Typical blog content is multi-media. The word count falls between 250 and 1000. Near the top, text flows left or right of a photo or two. Paragraphs are short. Often, a bulleted list stands-in for sentences. Further down, the writer invites comment and provides links to similar posts. You may find one last multi-media element at the bottom: the author's photo, accompanying a career-branded bio.

4. POST CONTENT FOR YOUR COMMUNITY

RESEARCHING CONTENT

Often, the facts and quotable wisdom needed for a blog post are a simple web search away. Strategic use of search operators[13] and relevant keywords make good googling.

- o You can focus results on one state using the search operator for location. For example, Lone Star State residents might include *location: TX* in their search strings.

- o Enclose multiple keywords, like "career development", in quotes. That way you will not have to wade through baseball career stats and housing development plans.

- o The *site* search operator brings results from the website that you specify. Try *"opportunity finder" site: jobkettle.com* to see ways the quoted term is used on that website.

- o Use the minus sign "-"to filter a word from results. Do not put a space between the minus and the word you wish to exclude. For example, *training –spring* will bring more results about classes and less about baseball.

- o The OR operator makes it possible to research two varied keywords at once.

- o When you want to find articles having every one of a list of terms, use the allintext search operator. Try *allintext: underemployment freeze jobless* to see pages that include all three of those keywords.

If you see the value in frequent, well-researched blogging, register on Alltop and NetworkedBlogs. Both are free, powerful blog search tools. Create browser bookmarks for both. They can save significant time in blog research.

o http://www.Alltop.com

Research over 32,000 blogs and news websites by category on Alltop.com. Using those same categories, you can create a free MyAlltop page.

Your MyAlltop page lists blog names with the five most recent headlines below each name. Click on the blog name to bring up its home page. When you hold (hover) the mouse pointer over an article title, a popup window displays the beginning of the article. Click the headline to retrieve the complete article.

o http://www.NetworkedBlogs.com

Use the topic directory to search blogs. Select the ones you'd like placed into content streams. Scroll across the NetworkedBlogs page to view one blog in each stream.

The streams display excerpts from posted content, with the most recent at the top. Excerpts include a headline, photo, and a few lines of text - all within a white rectangle. Click any rectangle to view the complete article, formatted for display within NetworkedBlogs.

FINDING GRAPHICS

Blog posts require at least one graphic. Most often, a photo is placed above or at the beginning of the text. The top photo automatically displays when the post is to Facebook, Google+, or LinkedIn.

Avoid using graphics that a search engine returns by keyword search. The search engine provider does not own those images, nor will you. It costs about a dollar to avoid copyright issues. For this small investment you can choose from millions of quality photos or drawings.

Keep costs minimal by choosing lower-resolution files. Unlike the banner graphics for Facebook and Twitter, most blog content requires no more than 72 dpi (dots per inch) and a width of 400 pixels. Smaller, low-resolution graphics cost less.

Try any of the online clip art and stock photo sources listed below in alphabetical order. Their internal search tools should bring up great photos or illustrations. Compare prices.

http://www.BigStockPhoto.com

http://www.Fotolia.com

http://www.iStockPhoto.com

http://www.ShutterStock.com

http://www.ThinkStockPhotos.com

Choose a photo or illustration that conveys a message similar to the headline. Imagine the headline as a caption to the graphic. If they match, both will invite further reading and sharing of the blog content. That's another way in which your online community grows!

DOCUMENTING SOURCES

Your helpful, shareable blog post may be based on content from across the web. It's okay to borrow. The one rule is that you must give credit and link to the original source. Qualify those fascinating facts and stunning statistics by assigning a footnote to each. If HTML tags like *<sup>* and *<a>* give you headaches, a WordPress plug in[14], FD Footnotes, automates the chore.

Keep track of Uniform Resource Locators (URL) as you research and write a blog post. When at the online source, copy the URL from the browser.

Often a link will seem long and ungainly, but you may be able to simplify it. If the URL includes a question mark, items to the right of it are *parameters*. Open another browser window and try the link without parameters. If the simplified URL brings up the page, it can be the source that you footnote.

CONTENT	Research the topic. Note at least two URL which you will cite as sources for the blog post.
	http://
	http://
	http://

Figure 24 – Blog Post Planning Worksheet (Content)

A declining number of bloggers will post entire articles written by another author. This is known as *guest blogging*.

It was once popular for authors to appear on many blogs, or for a blog to invite many authors. An online industry sprang up from this. For a fee, companies would maintain your blog with fresh but irrelevant content written by poorly-paid writers. Readers would not share this. The industry faded along with the practice of guest blogging.

CHOOSING A FORMAT

If you wisely avoid outsourcing your blog posts, the content you write can represent your professional brand. Keep that brand in mind as you choose a presentation style. Will you be teaching? Will you write factually or persuasively? Consider the options for sharing the topic in your voice.

Your brand/tag line:	

Check one or more ways to present the topic you chose, to reinforce your brand.

- ☐ Your teaching
- ☐ Your recommendations
- ☐ Your perspective
- ☐ Your reporting
- ☐ Your humor

Figure 25 – Blog Post Planning Worksheet (Presentation)

You have done your research. You know the subject. By now, this future blog post may be notes scratched on a yellow table, bullet points in a word processor, or random competing thoughts. It's time to choose a format.

If you like to write, a journalistic news article or review of the topic may be your best choice. If you have graphic flare (and the necessary software!), you may want to create a captioned photo gallery or digital scrapbook. Online tools like Piktochart[15] will to help you design an *infographic* from text and clip art.

Other format options keep writing to a minimum. Listicles are "list articles", a quick way to post the information you found. Listicles are easily recognized because they often have a number in their headline[16]. The greater the number, the less writing required! Numbers between 7 and 10 seem quite popular. Want proof? Try googling "10 ways".

Maybe your topic would be best presented through multimedia. That doesn't have to be expensive. LinkedIn offers Slideshare.net to help you upload infographics, documents, presentation decks, or videos. Slideshare includes an online tool for creating a presentation. A WordPress plugin[17] posts the results to your blog. It's all free!

FORMAT *Let content and the interests of your community determine your formatting decisions! Optionally, choose one from the list below:*

☐ News article	☐ Embedded video
☐ Review	☐ Gallery
☐ Interview	☐ Infographic
☐ Discussion	☐ Listicle
☐ How-to (recipe format)	☐ Scrapbook
☐ Q & A	☐ Slideshare

Obtain a public-domain graphic, or purchase from an online clip art library. This illustration will be near the top of your blog post.

File name of photo or drawing: ______

Figure 26 – Blog Post Planning Worksheet (Format)

Your blog post will need a headline. It is best to write this last, so that the headline accurately represents the blog post content.

Include at least one keyword from the article. This makes your article more likely to be retrieved by a Google, Bing, and other search engines. Resist the temptation to pack several keywords into the title. That makes the article less attractive to search engine and to the potential reader.

Don't suffer with writer's block over a simple headline. When in doubt, try one of these popular formats:

- The headline asks a question, where the blog post is the answer

  Looking for ways to cut operating expense?

  Is it time for an internal audit?

- The headline gives the number of key points in the listicle (list-based article)

  5 New Laws Every Accountant Must Know

  10 Best Tools for Corporate Tax Returns

o The headline begins with keywords followed by a colon

> Chart of Accounts: Best Practices for Small Business

> Business Intelligence for Accountants: The Essential Facts

Choose words that are bright and crisp. Favor the active voice over passive. Originality and humor are fine as long as the meaning remains clear.

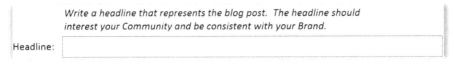

Write a headline that represents the blog post. The headline should interest your Community and be consistent with your Brand.

Headline:

Figure 27 – Blog Post Planning Worksheet (Content)

PLUGGING-IN

Blogging can be simple. A minimum of content plus a plugin or two yields a compelling post. You only have to write a few paragraphs and those are better brief than long.

Don't sweat the nouns and verbs. Instead, let technology provide the dazzle. If your WordPress blog is self-hosted over 30,000 plugins away.

o Surveys

Several plugins[18] will format a poll and graph the results. No programming is required. All you write is a question and possible responses. As individuals share their opinion, you learn about your online community.

o Quizzes

Will your blog post cover several facts? Consider a quiz plugin19 to introduce or summarize the topic. When you announce the quiz through Facebook or Twitter, potential readers will take up the challenge and visit your blog.

o Quotes

If your research unearths words of wisdom, choose from several hundreds of plugins[20] to emphasize those words. Quote experts in your profession, or beautifully present your original ideas.

o Contact forms

Readers may want to ask a question or receive a newsletter from you. Several plugins[21] will collect their names, addresses, and other information. Customize the form to gather needed information. Write responses or a newsletter as promised, then reach out to your online community.

o Social media buttons

Use plugins to promote sharing[22] on Facebook, Twitter, and more. Sharing is essential to social media marketing.

As you sample the vast array of free WordPress tools, you may encounter a scary problem. When overloaded by plugins, WordPress returns the "white screen of death". It will look like your blog is gone. Your browser displays a blank white screen.

The cure to this terrifying problem may be as easy as pausing to breathe deeply, drink a glass of cool water, then reload the page. If that doesn't work, browse to your domain URL, followed by */wp-admin.* With good luck, that brings up the dashboard. From the menu on the right side of the dashboard, select *Plugins*, then *Installed Plugins*. Deactivate the ones you most recently installed.

With bad luck, you have no access to the WordPress dashboard. Your blog remains behind that white screen. To again see it, summon the wisdom of the internet[23] or call your web hosting provider for technical support.

PROMOTING RESPONSE

Every blog post should end with a thoughtful question and your invitation to comment. Most themes give you control over this. Many include features to selectively publish comments. You may be able to thwart the anxious entrepreneurs who see your blog as free advertising space. Beware any unctuous or vague comments that praise your content. Do not click the links those comments invariably include. Disapprove. Delete. Purge.

Each topic on your list holds potential for one or more blog posts. You might write an article about it. Weeks later, the article might be adapted into a survey or quiz, powered by a WordPress plugin. Reuse your research. Recycle your invested time.

In chapter 3, you compared six social media services, matching them (in

Figure 19) to groups within your online community. Blog post topics also make great content for those social media services.

o Facebook

Announce your latest blog post in a status update. Ideal length is just enough to tantalize; 25 – 100 words. When you include a link, Facebook inserts a photo from the blog post.

o Google+

Flexible options offered by Google+ let you share photos, links, videos, and polls related to your blog. Start with a bolded headline. In the text, place asterisks before and after words you wish to emphasize, as in *I am open to opportunities*. A similar function, the underscore (_), puts the enclosed text in italics.

Google+ recommends use of hashtags. It automatically adds a few which you can select or replace. Want to go in-depth? Schedule a free *hangout* for online discussion.

o LinkedIn

To reach your connections, share updates on your LinkedIn home page. Hear about opportunities by joining groups that are specific to a career. For best exposure, be the person who initiates discussion with a probing question. Available options let you attach an image or other file, and simultaneously post to Twitter.

Group posts must be classified as *general*, *job*, or *promotion*. If your post includes a link to your blog, the group moderator may prefer that you share it as a *promotion*.

o Pinterest

Create or add to a pin board about your selected topic. Include a link to your blog in the description.

Your pins can include *.JPG*, *.PNG*, and *.GIF* images as well as videos in *YouTube*, *Vimeo* and *Ted* formats.

o Twitter

When you tweet about a blog post, consider adding a hashtag based on the topic. Use a link-trimming tool [24]to keep the total length within the 140-character limit.

o YouTube

Video content may be as simple as a *.MOV* file recorded on a cell phone. If the topic is relevant and the quality supports your professional brand, consider uploading content to your account. Accounts must be verified before upload of videos longer than 15 minutes or files larger than 128 gigabytes.

YouTube supports several formats:

3GPP

.AVI

.FLV

.MOV

.MP4

.MPEG4

.MPEGPS

WebM

.WMV

CHAPTER 4 RECAP

This chapter showed you how to plan, write, and share a blog post.

Planning begins with subjects from the chapter 3 Blog Options Worksheet. Arrange the subjects into categories, and list topics for each category.

Your popular blog should have fresh content each week, or more often. Begin by choosing an item from your Topic List. Research content for that topic and create or purchase at least one graphic to illustrate it. Protect copyrights by documenting and linking to all sources.

Choose a presentation style that fits your style and format the content to meet the interests of your online community. Do they favor factual articles? Write a news article, do a review, or interview an expert. Other formats are better for groups that favor visual content: galleries, infographics, and SlideShare presentations.

WordPress plugins allow you to insert surveys, quizzes, and quotes into a blog post. Though powerful, plugins can trigger the "white screen of death" if too many are selected. Only activate the plugins you need, and know how to deactivate the most recent ones.

Contact forms and social media buttons help to promote the content. Encourage discussion with a thoughtful question or ask for comment at the end. Bring the completed post to your groups through the social media services that they prefer.

CHAPTER 4 QUIZ

1. Which Google search string would be best for finding job interview information from the Forbes.com website, excluding interview questions?

   a) "job interview" – question @forbes.com

   b) Job + interview – question @forbes.com

   c) "job interview" -question site:forbes.coma

   d) "job interview" –"interview question" site:forbes.com

2. How could you use Google to find what the Pew Research Center wrote about underemployment in 2014?

   a) allintext: 2014 underemployment site:pewresearch.org

   b) @pewresearch.org +underemployment +2014

   c) 2014 underemployment @pewresearch.org

   d) All of the above

3. Which of the following statements about Alltop.com is false?

   a) For each news website or blog that it covers, Alltop displays the five most recent headlines.

   b) If you want multiple "MyAlltop" pages, you must set up multiple accounts

   c) To follow a feed, right-click the blog/news website name and select *Add to MyAlltop*

   d) The beginning of an article is displayed when a mouse pointer is hovered over it

4. If you want to create blog posts each week, what should you do first?

    a) Read current and relevant blogs that have a high Alexa rank

    b) Search Google news for blog posts, using the subject as a keyword

    c) Prepare a list of topics that relate to the subject of the blog

    d) At reddit.com, read the articles on the "top" and "rising" tabs

5. Which type of WordPress plugin would be most valuable in building an online community?

    a) Social media buttons, so more people will see your blog posts

    b) Quizzes, to directly involve your online community

    c) Surveys, for better understanding of your online community

    d) Quotes, to associate your work with experts in your profession

6. In a Google+ post, how could you italicize the job title of more than 4.4 million Americans?

    a) _Retail Salesperson_

    b) <i>Retail Salesperson</i>

    c) *Retail Salesperson*

    d) "Retail Salesperson"

7. What happens automatically in a Google+ post?

    a) The headline text is bolded

    b) Names mentioned in the text are hyperlinked to their profiles

    c) Hashtags are added

    d) All of the above

8. When open to new opportunities, what would be best to post in a LinkedIn group?

   a) A thoughtful comment in an existing General discussion

   b) An email address in a Promotion discussion

   c) A challenging question to begin a new General discussion

   d) A credential to begin a new Job discussion

9. Which video types are supported by Pinterest?

   a) TED, Vimeo, and YouTube

   b) MP3 and MP4

   c) SVI and RealMedia

   d) All of the above

10. What must you do before uploading a 20-minute video to YouTube?

    a) Verify your YouTube account

    b) Compress the file to less than 96 GB

    c) Convert the file to YouTube format

    d) None of the above

ANSWERS - CHAPTER 4 QUIZ

1. c   Quotes around "interview question" won't exclude "sample" or "behavioral" questions.

2. a   The allintext function returns results for the search terms which follow, in any order.

3. c   Alltop.com does not currently have "right-click" drop-down list functions.

4. c   As you begin a blog post, first choose a topic. This avoids "writer's block".

5. a   A community grows as one group member shares content to others with similar interests.

6. a   Enclose text in asterisks for emphasis, enclose with underscores for italics.

7. c   You can select or replace the hashtags which Google+ automatically adds to a post.

8. c   When your discussion thread draws comments, every participant sees your name.

9. a   Pinterest supports .JPG, .PNG, and .GIF images, plus TED, Vimeo, and YouTube video.

10. a   Account verification is required before uploading videos longer than 15 minutes.

Forms in This Chapter

Chapter 4 included these forms for developing social media content:

Content List Worksheet

Blog Post Planning Worksheet

Both forms are available in the *Job Seeker's Toolkit for Social Media Marketing*. Download the toolkit free at http://www.wagescope.com. All forms can be copied as needed, subject to terms explained in the toolkit.

5. MASTER SOCIAL MEDIA ENGAGEMENT

PREVIEW

Blogging and posting content is like "working the room" at a networking event. You shake hands with many team leaders and human resource professionals. They move through the crowd and shake other hands.

Months later, they have an opportunity perfectly matched to your professional brand. Will they remember you?

Individuals will remember you if you engage with them. Reach out to people in your online community. Engage with them through social media. They will learn your professional brand.

- Engage through social media. Find people who comment about or ask about topics relevant to your professional brand. Address their needs. Write responses that invite further sharing and further response.

- Log daily online activity. Keep track of where you search, what you find, and how you respond. Most responses should prove your professional brand rather than market it.

- Use power tools for social media engagement. Find individuals through keyword searches. Upload messages in bulk to be sent out at scheduled times. Maintain group lists, adding new contacts and removing inactive contacts.

RULES OF SOCIAL MEDIA ENGAGEMENT

Patient and persistent blogging and social media posts bring your content to an online community. In sharing, you introduce yourself. The quality of what you share reflects your professional brand.

Don't stop with an introduction. Extend your impact and grow your online community by engaging with individuals. Social media engagement *is*:

- o Finding great ideas and adding your perspective

- o Joining job-related discussions and sharing further ideas

- o Finding leaders and innovators, and asking intriguing questions

- o Discovering needs and offering answers

  Engagement *is not*:

- o A lecture

- o A debate

- o A billboard for your advertisements

Engagement requires listening and responding. Write as you would speak in friendly conversation. Stay on topic. Avoid blatant advertisement of your professional brand. Your hidden agenda should remain hidden.

Social media has few rules, but when engaging, remember the 80 – 20 rule. At least 80% of your posts, pins, comments, and tweets should contribute help, information, or a relevant perspective. No more than 20% of any online communication should be at all self-serving. Engagement is sharing, not selling... at least 80% of the time.

Know when *not* to engage. If you have no fresh ideas to contribute, withhold that stale response. If the thread is already too long, look elsewhere. If trolls are about and the discussion flares, step back from the flames.

Look for messages that are relevant to your professional brand. Read carefully before responding. Focus on the needs and perspectives of the individual. Remain positive and keep it brief.

Don't flatter the gurus and don't overwork the issue. Post a comment for a comment and a tweet for a tweet.

SHARING

With each engagement you, as an individual, reach out to another individual. It's like talking with a stranger. You are doing this to further your professional brand. Don't talk about the weather unless seeking opportunities as weather forecaster.

People respond to news that is positive and interesting. Always include a link to further information. Often, your blog should contain that information. People you engage with will appreciate that useful link and will enjoy reading your blog.

Members of your online community will respond to, even discuss, thought-provoking questions about their profession. Let them be the experts, too.

The 80 – 20 rule applies. For example, if an unemployed accountant were to search Twitter for *accountant Joplin*, several job listings might surface in the response stream. Before sending the inevitable link to a resume, the accountant should know more about the opportunity. A first tweet might ask, *does this involve corporate tax law?* and include a compressed[25] link to an article discovered through Google News.

The same response could be sent to several opportunities in that stream. Some would use *@username* to *reply* to the inquiring tax accountant. Before long, the hiring manager would ask for a resume.

A requested resume gets better attention than one piled on the desk. The 80 – 20 rule makes an outsider just a bit of an insider. The job candidate has been proven friendly, helpful, and knows something about what the hiring manager needs.

Engaging through social media provides an edge.

SERVICE SEARCHES

Engagement begins with a keyword search. Look for people who could benefit from what you have to share, based on what they post. Maybe they have a question and you have an answer. Maybe they have a vacancy to fill and you *are* the answer.

In the long-term, engagement furthers your professional brand. Choose keywords from your elevator speech summary (Figure 13). Type those words into the search box on any social media service. For current and active engagement, Google+ and Twitter are good places to start.

Singular versions of group names, like *recruiter* and *"hiring manager"*, also make productive keywords. They are especially valuable in job seeking. Consider all of your group names as possible keywords.

If a keyword is a trending topic or vital to your professional brand, try it alone as a Twitter *#hashtag*. That can launch a real-time conversation.

BLOG SEARCHES

You can also engage by responding to blog posts. The search tools[26] used in researching blog content are great for finding what other bloggers have written. Try using Google as well. The "Google Blog Search" tool is no longer offered[27], but similar results are available beginning at any Google search box. Above the returned results, click the *Search tools* option. This brings up further options to specify a time range or *Any time*, a type of result or *All results*, and a location.

Whether you search through blogs or social media services, log the keywords and hashtags that return best results. Reuse them the next time you engage online. Add new ones to the list.

SEARCHES		Facebook	Google+	LinkedIn	Pinterest	Twitter	YouTube	
Date	Blog (name)							Keywords/#Hashtags
		☐	☐	☐	☐	☐	☐	
		☐	☐	☐	☐	☐	☐	
		☐	☐	☐	☐	☐	☐	
		☐	☐	☐	☐	☐	☐	
		☐	☐	☐	☐	☐	☐	
		☐	☐	☐	☐	☐	☐	
		☐	☐	☐	☐	☐	☐	
		☐	☐	☐	☐	☐	☐	
		☐	☐	☐	☐	☐	☐	
		☐	☐	☐	☐	☐	☐	
		☐	☐	☐	☐	☐	☐	
		☐	☐	☐	☐	☐	☐	
		☐	☐	☐	☐	☐	☐	

Figure 28 – Daily Logs Worksheet (Searches)

RESPONDING

Glance over the results of your keyword searches. Focus on the items where your unique strengths and experience can help. Help might take the form of an answered question. You might share an online resource, or simply offer encouragement. Keep comments positive, because positive words build reputations while complaints and arguments build walls. Engagement is about building reputations. Where there is controversy, the best response may be no response.

Along with ways to comment, social media services provide ways to *endorse* or *support* individuals that you reach. A click to a word or icon sends feedback that builds friendships and encourages continued engagement.

o Facebook

When you click a *Like*, Facebook notifies the person who wrote the post. Your name is included in the list that drops down from the "thumbs-up" number. Hover a mouse pointer over the number to read the list.

The *Share* function is even more powerful. It offers options to copy the post to *your own timeline*, to *a friend's timeline*, to *a Facebook group*, or to *a Facebook page that you manage*. When you choose "On a page you manage", Facebook notifies the author that you shared the message. Your page gets content and the author sees your name.

o Google+

On the People and pages tab, Google+ shows images, *Add* buttons and *Follow* buttons. You can *add* individuals to circles, or *follow* pages that represent a storefront, service area, or brand.

The author can be added to Google+ circles. Hover over the name or the round photo to its left. A popup window includes an *Add* button with options to choose any number of circles. You can even *Create* a new circle with the author as its first member.

 The *+ number* button below a Google+ post shows how many people agree with or like the content. Click the button to increase that number and to notify the author.

 The *arrow* button to the right of the *plus* button shares the post to people or circles that you select. Again, the author is notified.

o LinkedIn

LinkedIn makes it easy to contact people and add new connections. *Follow* any group Discussions or Promotions to be informed of each new comment. Click an individual's name or photo to view their latest activity in that group. Following also provides a way to *Connect* that member to your online community.

It's easy to *Like* a Home page post or comment. The option also appears on Discussions and Promotions tabs of all groups.

Content can be shared many ways. *Share* updates with the public, or only with your connections. Post to selected groups where you are a member. Opportunities from the Jobs tab can also be shared to Twitter and Facebook.

The *Share Link* option, another way to share, is provided on group Promotions tabs.

o Pinterest

 The *Pin it* button reposts a graphic. When you use it in Pinterest or on a web browser[28], it notifies the person who originally posted the graphic. Consider setting up a pin board for content from your online community. Re-pinning engages individuals by letting them know their content was seen and appreciated.

o Twitter

Follow other Twitter users to include their messages in your Twitter stream. Often, those individuals will "follow back". That enables you to exchange Direct Messages (*DM*).

In Twitter, each tweet has a footer that includes tools to *favorite* or *retweet*. Either action engages other users when they learn that you have responded.

o YouTube

 On YouTube, click the icon below any video. The icon will *share* the video to Facebook, Google+, LinkedIn, Pinterest, Twitter, or any of eight other services.

The many buttons and options make it easy to engage through social media. On any day, you can initiate dozens of conversations. Log those conversations. That gives you a record of who you contacted, and when, and what you discussed.

Social media engagement happens one person at a time. It can be like meeting someone for a second time at a networking event. You can remember their name and what you discussed, or you can apologize.

An Engagement Log keeps the conversations going.

ENGAGEMENT

Date	Contact (name)	Service	Their interest/topic	Your response

Figure 29 - Daily Logs Worksheet (Engagement)

The five-column form works best as a Microsoft Excel spreadsheet. Type the five headings into row 1, columns A - E. Your Engagement Form now has room to grow. Click any heading, then select the ***Filter*** option found on Excel's Data tab. This adds a drop-down control to each heading. The control sorts and filters the form by *Contact (name)*, social media *Service*, or any other heading.

ENGAGING WITH POWER TOOLS

Engagement is searching and sharing online. Those basic functions can be fully accomplished through social media websites. Many services offer a smart phone app for small-screen engagement on the go. For a larger-screen view, bookmark the web addresses (URL) in any browser on your home computer.

When you engage, your social media community will respond. If response seems slow, take another look at the *power tools* you selected in chapter 3. Most can boost your engagement to reach more people and to better understand their needs.

o Klout

The *Klout Score* quantifies social media influence. Justin Bieber's "klout" registered at 100 while Barack Obama scored 92 and Mark Zuckerberg lagged with 81. Scores should grow in proportion with the size of an online community. Teen idols and career-minded professionals[29] can benefit from greater online influence. Politicians and corporate leaders may have less interest.

The score quantifies *influence*, not engagement[30]. Klout provides tools for searching and posting content to a Twitter or Facebook account. You can *schedule* a post for one future date and time.

o HootSuite

A free HootSuite account provides *one-time scheduling*. An upgrade to Pro status enables *bulk-scheduling*. You can schedule tweets for many future dates and times, but each must be unique. Twitter will reject repeated tweets.

A free account provides *one-time scheduling*.

Want to post to several services at once? HootSuite displays Facebook, Google+, LinkedIn, and Twitter search results in *streams*, side-by-side.

Keyword search can be limited within a fixed distance of specified geocodes. For example, a HootSuite user could:

Select the Joplin, Missouri City Hall in Google Maps. That places a marker on the map and includes latitude and longitude in the browser address bar.

Cut, paste, and reformat the latitude and longitude as a geocode that includes a distance in kilometers – geocode:37.0852716,-94.5137796, 75km

Search for Tweets sent from within 75 kilometers of the Joplin, Missouri City Hall.

Access the *Quick Search* function by clicking an hourglass icon. This enables a *crosshairs* icon which adds a parameter to return results within 25 kilometers of your location. You can edit and save parameters as a stream.

HootSuite also displays Twitter lists, including three useful numbers: *Following*, *Followers*, and *Klout* score. One click of a push button will *Follow* or *Unfollow* anyone on the list.

o Listly

Many blogs contain lists. Often, a list is by one person and only that person can edit it. Listly adds a social dimension. Individuals change list order by ranking items up or down. They also can add items to a list. The owner has the option to curate it, approving any new items.

Share a list to your online community through Facebook, Google+, LinkedIn, or Twitter. They can then *Follow* and further share it.

After registering[31], install the Listly extension[32] in your Google Chrome browser. With it, each web page can be list content. Add items or create new lists directly from the browser.

o Topsy[33]

Topsy helps you engage with influential social media users. It finds the most popular online messages and handles your *reply* or *retweet*.

On an average day, Twitter's 232 million active users send out a half-billion tweets. Topsy mines this gargantuan data pile. It extracts tweets, using keyword searches plus advanced filters:

Tweets having links to specific websites

Tweets containing photos or video

Tweets being shared

A search string becomes a topic. Topics are given a *Sentiment Score*, with 50 being neutral and 0 as most negative, 100 as most positive. The *universe* scores 83 and the lowly *cockroach* gets 21.

Social Trends displays tweets, webpage links, photos, and videos for the most popular conversations about a topic.

Social Search returns the most recent tweets, links, photos, videos, and influencers of a topic. Results include counts for the previous hour, day, week, and month.

Social Analytics produces a 30-day graph for terms within a search string. As you plan social media engagement, you can see which keywords elicit the greatest number of responses.

o TweetAdder

Most social media power tools are browser-based. One exception, TweetAdder, must be installed[34] on a Mac or Windows desktop computer.

The *Follow Back List* shows Twitter accounts that follow you. Move ones that you do not wish to immediately follow to the *Follow Later List*.

You may wish to discontinue following a Twitter account. TweetAdder helps you *unfollow users not following back* and those who *unfollowed you*. Another option will *blacklist* unwanted followers.

TweetAdder provides advanced *Search* functions. Each includes the ability to specify a range (in miles):

Profile Data Search

Find people locally or at any range, based on what they have written about themselves in their Twitter profile.

Location Search and Tweet Search

These functions are similar to the keyword search available in Twitter. TweetAdder also lets you filter results by how far, how recent, and how popular each tweet has been.

Other TweetAdder engagement tools search for *Followers of User* or accounts that are *Followed by a User*.

TweetAdder limits free use to 3 days before charging $19 per month. Individual Klout accounts are free. When using any of the other power tools, be prepared for tempting upgrade offers.

POWER TOOL	FEATURES	COST TO UPGRADE	UPGRADES
HootSuite	• Up to 3 profiles • Single message scheduling	$9.95/month	• Up to 50 profiles • Bulk message scheduling
Klout	• Klout score • Single message scheduling • Search tools	No upgrades	
List.ly	• Unlimited lists and items • Google Chrome extension	$9.99/month	• Premium layouts • No adds on lists
Topsy	• Search social trends • Social analytics	No upgrades for private accounts	
TweetAdder	• Free trial (3 days/complete)	$19/month	• Location search • Profile data search • Find followers of a user • Find followed by a user

Figure 30 – Power Tool Upgrades

AUTOMATION STRATEGIES

All of the Power Tools will post content for you. For example, you might:

o Direct blog posts (through an .RSS feed) from a valued source to your own blog, using HootSuite

o Schedule an update to your Facebook page at a time recommended by Klout

o Add items to a Twitter list, using Listly

o Retweet links and images from key influencers, using Topsy

o Use TweetAdder to post messages and links every 45 to 55 minutes, 20 times per day

When you schedule content, take another few seconds to log that activity. The log will track how much content each power tool brings to your online community.

SCHEDULED CONTENT				HootSuite	Klout	Listly	Topsy	TweetAdder	
Date	Topic		Service						Quantity
				☐	☐	☐	☐	☐	
				☐	☐	☐	☐	☐	
				☐	☐	☐	☐	☐	
				☐	☐	☐	☐	☐	
				☐	☐	☐	☐	☐	
				☐	☐	☐	☐	☐	
				☐	☐	☐	☐	☐	
				☐	☐	☐	☐	☐	
				☐	☐	☐	☐	☐	

Figure 31 – Automation Strategies (Scheduled Content)

You should also track when and how you use power tools. That information will become part of your monthly *analytics* (discussed in Chapter 6). Over time, this can be matched to *analytics* (discussed in Chapter 6) to assess the value of each tool and strategy.

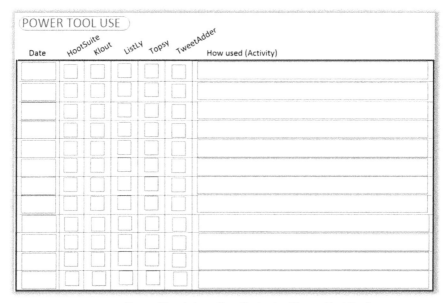

Figure 32 – Automation Strategies (Power Tool Use)

CHAPTER 5 RECAP

Social media engagement is *finding* and *sharing*. It begins when you find individuals who have interests or needs relevant to your professional brand. In response, you share information or join in a discussion. Sometimes you reach out with encouragement.

Marketing may follow, since 80% of your online communication should be helpful, informative, or amusing and no more than 20% should be self-promotion.

Social media services provide search functions. Keep a log of the keywords you use. Reuse keywords that lead to individuals who could benefit from your information or help. Those people should be in a group within your online community.

Social media services also provide one-click tools for showing agreement, following, or sharing the content posted by others. These lead to engagement which further builds a community.

Several power tools automate and extend social media services. Find people within a distance that you specify. Write content in advance and have it posted when and where it will most likely be read. Most tools are free or low-cost but can return even greater value if you log when and how you use them.

CHAPTER 5 QUIZ

1. What is the "80-20 rule" for social media marketing?

    a) 80% help, inform, or ask a relevant question. Less than 20% anything self-serving.

    b) 80% writing new content; 20% sharing existing content

    c) 80% posting to Twitter; 20% posting to other social media services

    d) 80% engaging through social media services; 20% posting to a blog

2. What is essential when commenting on a blog post?

    a) Before writing anything, thoroughly read the original post. Limit your response to that same topic.

    b) Prepare time-saving "boilerplate" responses. Adapt each response for use on as many blogs as possible.

    c) When you have strong feelings about a subject, don't pretend to be neutral. Share what you know about that subject.

    d) Focus on your professional brand and include a link to your blog.

3. What should you do in response to an extreme, controversial blog post?

    a) Be clear and positive in responding to the post

    b) If you have a different perspective, share it so people can see both sides

    c) Include hyperlinks to less-controversial, more accurate material

    d) It is better not to respond

4. How searches for recent blog entries done at Google.com?

   a) From the search box, using Search tools

   b) From the search box, using the *source:blog* function

   c) From *blogs.google.com*

   d) From *blogsearch.google.com*

5. What is the most effective search strategy for current job openings?

   e) Use the #job, #hiring, and #recruit hashtags on LinkedIn

   a) On Twitter, use the name of your profession and your town or city as keywords

   b) On LinkedIn, search company pages for jobs in your profession

   c) Schedule hourly tweets using HootSuite. Each tweet should ask about opportunities and include a link to your resume.

6. Which of these can be viewed in HootSuite without installing an app?

   a) Google+ circles

   b) RSS feeds from self-hosted blogs

   c) YouTube videos

   d) None of the above

7. Which is not possible with Listly?

   a) Indenting list items as an outline

   b) Embedding a list on a blog

   c) Sharing a list on Facebook and Twitter

   d) Sharing a list on LinkedIn

8. How could you find tweets about employment as a chef in or near Dayton, Ohio?

   a) In Twitter, search using #chef and #dayton hashtags.

   b) In TweetAdder, search with the job title as keyword. Input the location and leave the default distance.

   c) In HootSuite, use a quick search for *chef* and choose the geocode icon.

   d) Create a list of Dayton, Ohio chefs in Twitter. Create a stream for it in HootSuite.

9. What specific tweets can be searched using Topsy?

   a) Tweets having links

   b) Tweets having photos

   c) Tweets having videos

   d) All of the above

10. How can a Direct Message (*DM*) be sent to a Twitter user?

   a) Include *@username* at the beginning of the tweet

   b) Begin the tweet with *DM*, followed by *@username* of the recipient

   c) HootSuite and TweetAdder enable *DM* with any Twitter user

   d) After any two users follow each other, either one can *DM* the other

ANSWERS - CHAPTER 5 QUIZ

1. a   Advertisements and promotional posts are avoided. Useful information is shared.

2. a   Engagement in social media is one-to-one. To stay on topic, read before responding.

3. d   Complaints and arguments build walls. Engagement is about building reputations.

4. a   The search tools can limit results by time and location

5. b   Employers often tweet their location and a job title when looking for candidates.

6. a   Google+ can be added as a social network in HootSuite.

7. a   The Listly plugin can be used to create, curate, or collaborate.

8. b   The default distance for a Tweet Search in TweetAdder is 25 miles.

9. d   Tweets having links, photos, and videos can all be found using Topsy.

10. a   Direct Messages (DM) are not delivered unless both users have followed each other.

FORMS IN THIS CHAPTER

Chapter 5 included these forms to support efficient and wide-ranging social media outreach:

Daily Logs (Search and Engagement)

Automation Strategies Worksheet

The forms are available in the *Job Seeker's Toolkit for Social Media Marketing*. Download the toolkit free at http://www.wagescope.com. All forms can be copied as needed, subject to terms explained in the toolkit.

6. REFINE YOUR MARKETING PLAN

Your online community is growing and changing. Are you changing with it, or will it grow elsewhere?

Each social media service invites response in varied yet simple ways. Know which blog topics and engagement channels have the greatest impact.

As your "klout" increases, you may invest more time and buy upgraded services. Get the best return from every hour and dollar invested in social media.

- Each month, track your social media marketing success. Know the significant metrics of the social media services you used. Set up analytics on Google, HootSuite, or Klout. Gage the response that your online community has to your professional brand.
- Maintain your blog dashboard. Moderate responses. Review dashboard analytics
- Track current and to date outreach and response. Log your social media service activity. Total the responses you have seen this month and to date.
- Update your Social Media Marketing Plan. Decide which social media services and power tools to use more or less.

REFINING YOUR REACH

Change is the only constant[35] in social media. Technologies evolve. Web services add and deprecate features. Business priorities evolve. Members of your online community will change professions, just as you may.

To maintain engagement, know how the people you engage *currently* respond to your blog posts and social media outreach. Measure and evaluate:

o Which content is most appreciated?

People may write flattering comments about a blog post. They may click a *Like* or *Favorite* button on a social media service. These actions show appreciation, but the most-appreciated content will be *shared* on Facebook, Google+, and LinkedIn. Your valued professional brand will be *followed* on Pinterest and Twitter. It will be *subscribed to* on YouTube.

o Which services are most popular with each group?

Individuals may decide one service takes too much time, and another better suits their needs. New advertising may frustrate some or they may dislike a new rule. In any of those conditions, they no longer visit where they once posted daily.

o Which groups are the most responsive?

In chapter 2, you chose the groups to reach through social media. Some group members will engage through comments and Direct Messages (DM). Know which groups consistently engage. For other groups, different strategies may be needed.

Allocate time between social media channels based on what people want to read, where they want to read it, and who most often responds. Scale up or scale back power tool use as needed. Reach the right people through the right media.

USING ANALYTICS

Social media services produce extensive and varied data.

o *Insights* are available to any Facebook page administrator. One click brings up *page likes*, *post reach*, and *engagement*.

o The *Pages* option in Google+ retrieves the *number of followers* and *date of last post*.

o Counts on the LinkedIn home page reveal how often your *profile* has been viewed and the number of *connections* in your network. You should also track the number of people in any LinkedIn groups that you manage. That count is the best measure of your influence. As your influence grows, your professional brand strengthens.

o The home page at Pinterest presents an array of counts: *boards*, *pins*, *likes*, *followers*, and *following*.

o At the Twitter website, you immediately see how many *tweets* you have sent, counts of people you are *following*, and how many are *following* you.

o The YouTube Creator Studio displays Channel Stats with *views*, *estimated minutes watched* and *subscribers* for the past 28 days

Analytics will retrieve and reformat data from multiple services. Create custom reports and graphics that go far beyond rows and columns of numbers. Trace history in a line, or compare results between columns. Easily discover trends and highlights of your social media marketing.

Google supports extensive analytics of a blog and the social media referrals to that blog. The only cost for Google Analytics is time. Setup requires patience and computer skills. You will need a need a free Google account[36]. At the home page for analytics[37] launch the new account process by clicking *Access Google Analytics*. This brings up several questions about your blog website. Based on your answers, Google creates a tracking ID which can only be installed on a self-hosted[38] blog.

An easier route to analytics brings limited information directly to the dashboard of a self-hosted WordPress blog. If you are mostly interested in visitor counts and pages per visit, install the Google Analytics Plugin[39] and then the Google Analytics Dashboard Plugin[40].

HootSuite offers analytics through detailed customized reports. These present data pulled from your blog and social media services, formatted as pie charts, graphs, sparklines[41], and map overlays. View that data as plan-text numbers and percentages, if you prefer. The *Free* plan is limited to three basic reports. The *Pro* plan also includes one fully-configurable advanced report.

Klout provides score analytics from a main menu selection. When you choose *Measure,* a *90 Day Score History* appears as a graph. *Network Contribution* percentages below it are based on recent Twitter, Facebook page, Google+, and LinkedIn updates. Individual tabs further analyze how each service contributes to the scores.

Use any or all Google, HootSuite, and Klout analytics based on your available time and budget.

MAINTAINING A BLOG

Social media marketing brings results, month after month. Begin your monthly assessment of those results at the dashboard of your WordPress.com or self-hosted blog. View the counts for posts and comments *at a glance*. Look below *Activity* to verify the dates and headlines of recent posts. Is the blog current? Fresh content invites an online community to it again and again.

The thick black ribbon at the dashboard's left edge is a vertical menu. Look for *update* numbers in red circles. Click any red circles that you see to install updates for plugins and themes.

Moderate pending comments. This involves approving valid ones and moving the others[42] to trash. The valid ones also merit brief relevant replies. Replies continue the online conversation, also known as engagement.

Before closing the comment list, click the *Empty Trash* button. The count of *pending* comments should now be zero.

MEASURING OUTREACH

Links that you include in posts, pins, comments, and tweets will bring an online community to your blog[43]. Measure your outreach each month. Keep a log of social media services and functions that you used to reach out.

In most cases, individual services display post and follower counts as totals *to date*. In the log you keep, subtract the previous month's total from this month's amount.   That gives you a *current* count. The numbers may or may not change, month to month but if you have used the service, you should see responses.

Used (Y/N)	Service	Outreach	# Current	# To Date
OUTREACH		From / /	Through / /	
☐	Facebook	Comments made		
☐	Facebook	Posts shared (others)		
☐	Google+	People in your circles		
☐	Google+	Posts shared (others)		
☐	LinkedIn	Connections		
☐	LinkedIn	Groups belonged to		
☐	LinkedIn	Following		
☐	LinkedIn	Posts made		
☐	LinkedIn	Posts shared (others)		
☐	LinkedIn	Comments made		
☐	Pinterest	Pin boards		
☐	Pinterest	Pins you added		
☐	Pinterest	Pins you liked		
☐	Pinterest	Pinners you follow		
☐	Twitter	Tweets sent		
☐	Twitter	Tweets you retweeted		
☐	Twitter	PM sent		
☐	YouTube	Videos		
☐	YouTube	Videos shared (others)		
☐	YouTube	Comments (other videos)		
☐	YouTube	Subscriptions		

Figure 33 – Engagement Log

MEASURING RESPONSE

As you track *outreach*, do the same for the *response* you receive. Social media service websites count *shares*, *retweets*, and similar responses to individual posts. For monthly totals, use Klout, HootSuite, or any of your favorite power tools.

Look at last month's *Response* form as you complete this month's. Subtract responses *to date* from the previous total. The result is a *current* count.

RESPONSE			From	/ /	Through	/ /
Used (Y/N)	Service	Response			# Current	# To Date
☐	Facebook	Comments (your posts)				
☐	Facebook	Shares (your posts)				
☐	Facebook	Likes (your page)				
☐	Google+	Shares (your posts)				
☐	Google+	Views				
☐	Google+	Have you in circles				
☐	LinkedIn	Group members (total)				
☐	LinkedIn	Followers (total)				
☐	LinkedIn	Comments (your posts)				
☐	LinkedIn	Shares (your posts)				
☐	Pinterest	Pins others liked (your boards)				
☐	Pinterest	Pins others added (your boards)				
☐	Pinterest	Pinners following you (total)				
☐	Twitter	Mentions				
☐	Twitter	Retweeted by others				
☐	Twitter	PM received				
☐	YouTube	Comments (your videos)				
☐	YouTube	Views				
☐	YouTube	Subscribers (total)				

Figure 34 – Response Log

UPDATING YOUR PLAN

Armed with current data about blog and social media service performance, it's time to update your Social Media Marketing Plan.

With so many graphs and charts available, the detail can be overwhelming. If you're focused on growth, *follows* will matter more than *likes*. When reinforcing a professional brand, *mentions* mean more than *retweets*. For each service, evaluate one or two **metrics** that are most relevant to your campaign.

| SERVICES | | | | | |
Service	Approx. hours/week	Metric	Results	Trend	Planned hours/week
Facebook					
Google+					
LinkedIn					
Pinterest					
Twitter					
YouTube					

Figure 35 – Decisions Worksheet (Services)

As you approximate **hours** spent and assess **results** achieved consider rebalancing your overall efforts:

o Posting.

   If few people read your eloquent blog, you may want to write fewer posts and engage more through searching and responding.

109

o Searching.

A misdirected search leads to people with no interest in your professional brand. Update your Daily Logs Worksheet[44] with new keywords.

On the other hand, a search might seem *too* successful. Does your community inundate you in a flood of comments and questions? Take some time from searching and apply it to responding.

o Responding.

Your online community will further grow through retweets, "plus-ones", shares, and mentions. When that happens, shift more time to responding. Keep new members in your community with prompt follow-up to their comments and questions.

In fine-tuning your use of power tools, review the *features used* and *results* achieved. Decide on your *planned use* of the tools next month.

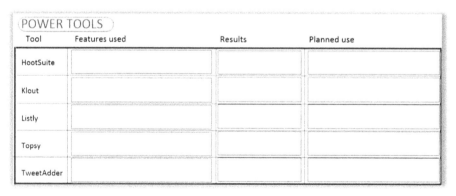

| POWER TOOLS | | | |
Tool	Features used	Results	Planned use
HootSuite			
Klout			
Listly			
Topsy			
TweetAdder			

Figure 36 – Decisions Worksheet (Power Tools)

ENJOYING SUCCESS

Each month, as you review analytics and evaluate results, look through the earlier worksheets as well. You will likely change a few words from time to time. Kept current, the worksheets are a framework for social media marketing, from start to success:

o Plan a campaign

Goal Development Worksheet

Marketing Plan

o Create a professional brand

Community Planning Worksheet

Brand Development

o Claim your territory

Blog Options Form

Services Options Form

o Post content for your community

Content List

Blog Post Planning Worksheet

o Master social media engagement

Daily Logs

Automation Strategies Worksheet

o Refine your marketing plan

Engagement and Response Logs

Service and Power Tool Decision Forms

Whether jobless and just starting out, or employed and in the corner office, engage with your online community. Discover needs and share from your experience.

Be the expert. Further your professional brand through social media. Stay current in your professional skills and find the latest opportunities.

Enjoy every benefit of social media marketing.

Chapter 6 Recap

A marketing plan sets a path through social media's shifting landscape. You must update the map as web services offer new services, and the priorities of your online community evolve.

Keep track of social media engagement. Know which content is most appreciated, which services are most popular, and which groups are most responsive. Track the time you spend and the results you see through social media services. Fine tune your use of power tools.

Maintain your blog dashboard. Is it time for another post? Moderate pending comments. Reply to valid comments, move the others to trash.

Analytics document blog and social media service responses through reports, charts, and graphs. Google offers all of these after installation of a tracking ID. Once in place, Google Analytics are a powerful resource. HootSuite and Klout offer more convenient solutions. Beyond the free basic services, the more advanced features are only available after paid upgrades.

CHAPTER 6 QUIZ

1. What does it mean to *moderate* blog comments?

    a) Limit the number of comments added to your blog post

    b) When writing comments, avoid extremes in opinion and emotion

    c) Promptly respond to any issues or complaints

    d) Delete any "spam" comments and empty the deleted "trash"

2. Which Facebook feature has the greatest value for building a professional brand?

    a) Comments

    b) Posts shared with the public

    c) Posts shared to a timeline

    d) Likes

3. When you look at your Google+ results, what should you track?

    a) How many times each of your pages is viewed

    b) How many people have you in their circles

    c) How many people have one of your pages in their circles

    d) All of the above

4. Which count best shows your growing influence on LinkedIn?

    a) Profile views

    b) Employer recommendations

    c) Members in the groups you manage

    d) Connections

5. What is greatest value provided by a social media journal?

   a) Associating hiring managers with the companies where they work

   b) Knowledge of which days of the week are best for social media use

   c) Strategies for placing ads and promoting content

   d) Better allocation of time between social media channels

6. What is required to configure your blog for Google Analytics?

   a) The Google Analytics and Google Analytics Dashboard plugins

   b) A tracking code number

   c) Tracking code script to paste into blog pages

   d) All of the above

7. What *insights* are available to a Facebook page administrator?

   a) Page follows and shares

   b) Comment counts

   c) Page likes, post reach, and engagement

   d) All of the above

8. Why is it important to review search terms each month?

   a) Searching should not take longer than responding

   b) You may be reaching people with no interest in your professional brand

   c) For best results, experiment with new keywords

   d) All of the above

9. What additional investment is recommended as an online community grows?

    a) Configure up to 50 social media profiles In HootSuite

    a) Create custom HootSuite reports

    b) Upgrade web hosting to handle greater volume of blog visitors

    c) Invest more time engaging with more people

10. How can successful engagement be measured?

    a) Keep a log of the Outreach that was done

    b) Keep a log of Responses that were received

    c) Subtract last month's *To Date* totals from this month's

    d) All of the above

ANSWERS - CHAPTER 6 QUIZ

1. d Unwanted comments should be deleted and the trash emptied each month.

2. b A post publicly shared is seen by friends who currently engage with the person who shared it.

3. d The Response Log has spaces to record those counts.

4. c As your influence grows, your professional brand strengthens.

5. d Together, the Engagement and Response logs show which outreach was most productive.

6. a During configuration, the plugins obtain and install the necessary tracking codes.

7. c One click brings up page likes, post reach, and engagement.

8. b A misdirected search leads to people with no interest in your professional brand.

9. d Prompt follow-up will keep new members in your community.

10. d Engagement is the response received for the outreach that was done, month after month.

FORMS IN THIS CHAPTER

Chapter 6 included these forms for monthly analysis and planning of social media activity:

Engagement Log

Response Log

Decisions Worksheet

These forms are available in the *Job Seeker's Toolkit for Social Media Marketing*. Download the toolkit free at http://www.wagescope.com. All forms can be copied as needed, subject to terms explained in the toolkit.

ABOUT THE AUTHOR

George is a Job Hunter for JobKettle.com. Armed with keyboard and mouse, he captures opportunities in 676 career fields.

After a prosaic career in public school music, George retreated to technical writing, programming and training development for Computer Sciences Corp. and the Walt Disney World Co. More recently, he consulted as Business Analyst and Technical Writer for Fortune 500 companies in and around Central Florida.

He now blogs, tweets, and posts full-time. Reach him at WageScope.com or send a tweet to @wagescope.

NOTES AND LINKS

1 http://jobsearch.about.com/od/employmentinformation/f/change-jobs.htm

2 http://en.wikipedia.org/wiki/List_of_social_networking_websites

3 http://money.usnews.com/money/blogs/outside-voices-careers/2014/09/17/dont-believe-these-8-job-search-myths

4 http://www.quora.com/How-much-does-Topsy-Pro-Analytics-costs

5 http://job-websites.findthebest.com/l/61/CareerBuilder-LLC

6 http://stylecaster.com/best-free-blog-sites/

7 "14 Surprising Statistics about WordPress Usage" Tom Ewer. Manage WP Blog 2/7/2014 https://managewp.com/14-surprising-statistics-about-wordpress-usage

8 http://theme.wordpress.com/themes/features/responsive-layout/?sort=free

9 http://www.creativebloq.com/web-design/free-wordpress-themes-712429

10 http://www.pcmag.com/article2/0,2817,2407168,00.asp

11 https://www.facebook.com/setting

12 https://twitter.com/settings/security

13 https://support.google.com/websearch/answer/136861

14 https://wordpress.org/plugins/fd-footnotes/

15 http://piktochart.com/

16 http://www.theguardian.com/media/shortcuts/2013/sep/01/11-reasons-why-still-love-listicles

17 https://wordpress.org/plugins/slideshare/

18 https://wordpress.org/plugins/search.php?q=poll

19 https://wordpress.org/plugins/search.php?q=quiz

20 https://wordpress.org/plugins/search.php?q=quotes

21 https://wordpress.org/plugins/search.php?q=contact+form

22 https://wordpress.org/plugins/search.php?q=social+media+button

23 Visit google.com and enter the keywords "WordPress white screen of death", or try https://thethemefoundry.com/blog/wordpress-white-screen-of-death/

24 See http://www.tinyurl.com or http://www.bit.ly

25 See http://www.tinyurl.com or http://www.bit.ly

26 Alltop and NetworkedBlogs

[27] http://googlecode.blogspot.com/2011/05/spring-cleaning-for-some-of-our-apis.html

[28] https://help.pinterest.com/en/articles/add-pin-it-button-your-browser#Web

[29] Register at http://www.klout.com to learn your score and read ways to boost it. No teenage antics required.

[30] Chapter 6 covers ways to measure engagement.

[31] Register at http://list.ly/

[32] https://chrome.google.com/webstore/search/listly

[33] Owned by Apple, Inc. http://www.crunchbase.com/organization/topsy-labs

[34] Free download from http://tweetadder.com/download/

[35] Long before social media, the Greek philosopher Heraclitus observed that everything changes and
nothing stands still. "You cannot step twice into the same river."
Scattered writings; circa 504 BC.

[36] https://accounts.google.com/signupwithoutgmail

[37] http://www.google.com/analytics/

[38] Chapter 3 discusses differences between self-hosted WordPress blogs and those hosted at WordPress.com

[39] https://wordpress.org/plugins/google-analytics-for-wordpress/

[40] https://wordpress.org/plugins/google-analytics-dashboard/

[41] *Sparklines* are small line charts. They lack the axes and coordinates seen on larger charts.

[42] Chapter 4 has more about the vague, flattering comments often seen on blog posts.

[43] Chapter 5 explains this in further detail.

[44] Explained in chapter 5

www.ingramcontent.com/pod-product-compliance
Lightning Source LLC
Chambersburg PA
CBHW070836070326
40690CB00009B/1569